CREATIVITY
and
INNOVATION:

The ASTD Trainer's Sourcebook

D1506874

Books in The ASTD Trainer's Sourcebook Series

Elaine Biech
CREATIVITY AND INNOVATION: THE ASTD TRAINER'S SOURCEBOOK

Anne F. Coyle
LEADERSHIP: THE ASTD TRAINER'S SOURCEBOOK

Dennis C. Kinlaw
COACHING: THE ASTD TRAINER'S SOURCEBOOK

Dennis C. Kinlaw
FACILITATION SKILLS: THE ASTD TRAINER'S SOURCEBOOK

Lisa McLain
PROJECT MANAGEMENT: THE ASTD TRAINER'S SOURCEBOOK

Herbert R. Miller
SALES: THE ASTD TRAINER'S SOURCEBOOK

Tina Rasmussen
DIVERSITY: THE ASTD TRAINER'S SOURCEBOOK

Sean T. Ryan
CUSTOMER SERVICE: THE ASTD TRAINER'S SOURCEBOOK

Judson Smith
QUALITY: THE ASTD TRAINER'S SOURCEBOOK

Cresencio Torres & Deborah M. Fairbanks
TEAM BUILDING: THE ASTD TRAINER'S SOURCEBOOK

Bobette Hayes Williamson
SUPERVISION: THE ASTD TRAINER'S SOURCEBOOK

John C. Wills
STRATEGIC PLANNING: THE ASTD TRAINER'S SOURCEBOOK

CREATIVITY and INNOVATION:

The ASTD Trainer's Sourcebook

Elaine Biech

35. 29

McGraw-Hill

New York San Francisco Washington D.C. Auckland Bogotá
Caracas Lisbon London Madrid Mexico City Milan
Montreal New Delhi San Juan Singapore
Sydney Tokyo Toronto

Library of Congress Catalog Card Number: 96-75330

McGraw-Hill

A Division of The McGraw·Hill Companies

STATEMENT OF COPYRIGHT AND REPRODUCIBILITY

TRADEMARKS:

PERMISSIONS:

1 2 3 4 5 6 7 8 9 MAL/MAL 9 0 1 0 9 8 7 6

ISBN 0-07-053445-4

Sourcebook Team:

Co-Publishers:	Philip Ruppel, McGraw-Hill Training
	Nancy Olson, American Society for Training and Development
Acquisitions Editor:	Richard Narramore, McGraw-Hill Training
Editing Supervisor:	Paul R. Sobel, McGraw-Hill Professional Book Group
Production Supervisor:	Donald F. Schmidt, McGraw-Hill Professional Book Group
Series Advisor:	Richard L. Roe
Illustrated by:	Claire Condra Arias
Editing/Imagesetting:	Claire Condra Arias, Stacy Marquardt, Ellipsys International Publications, Inc.
	Kalista Johnston-Nash

this book is dedicated
to all kreative kids
everywhere
...no matter what
your age
and especially
for two fine kids
Thad and Shane
who colored my
world
creative

Contents

Preface

I'd like to tell you how this series came about. As a long-time editor and resource person in the field of human resources development, I was frequently asked by trainers, facilitators, consultants, and instructors to provide them with training designs on a variety of topics. These customers wanted one-hour, half-day, and full-day programs on such topics as team-building, coaching, diversity, supervision, and sales. Along with the training designs, they required facilitator notes, participant handouts, flipchart ideas, games, activities, structured experiences, overhead transparencies, and instruments. But, that wasn't all. They wanted to be able to reproduce, customize, and adapt these materials to their particular needs—at no cost!

Later, as an independent editor, I shared these needs with Nancy Olson, the publisher at the American Society for Training and Development. Nancy mentioned that ASTD received many similar calls from facilitators who were looking for a basic library of reproducible training materials. Many of the classic training volumes, such as Newstrom and Scannell's *Games Trainers Play* provided a variety of useful activities. However, they lacked training designs, handouts, overheads, and instruments—and, most importantly, they tended to be organized by method rather than by topic. You can guess the rest of the story: Welcome to *The ASTD Trainer's Sourcebook*.

This sourcebook is part of an open-ended series that covers the training topics most often found in many organizations. Instead of locking you into a prescribed "workbook mentality," this sourcebook will free you from having to buy more workbooks each time you present training. This volume contains everything you need—background information on the topic, facilitator notes, training designs, participant handouts, activities, instruments, flipcharts, overheads, and resources—and it's all reproducible! We welcome you to adapt it to your particular needs. Please read the copyright limitations on page iv, then photocopy. . . edit . . . add your name . . . add your client's name. Please don't tell us . . . it isn't necessary! Enjoy.

Richard L. Roe
ASTD Sourcebook Series Advisor

Thank you to. . .

Everyone in the office for their support.

Beth Drake, Sonya Zimmerman, Robin Lucas, DC Campbell, and Lori Skeels for your support in a hundred ways.

Sherri Slack whose ideas from our first effort influenced and inspired me for this book. Dan Greene whose creative ideas never seem to end.

Claire Condra Arias who added class to our creative chaos, turning a flat paper manuscript into a dynamic living resource.

Chapter One:

Why Creativity?

Creativity: Why is it important? What is it?

The first question is difficult to answer; the second nearly impossible!

WHAT'S IN THIS CHAPTER?

This chapter examines the historical, physical, personal, and professional aspects of creativity—providing background information, strategies and techniques to enhance your presentation.

Businesses Need Creativity

It seems like all companies have recently gone mad! Why?

If your company is like most, you are going through many changes. Your company may have recently invested in state-of-the-art technology. It may have plans to broaden its customer base. It may be expanding into foreign countries. It may have redesigned the business processes by which it operates. It may have flattened, delayered, teamed, reengineered, process improved or reorganized.

It changed. And, along with that change comes problems—new problems that require new solutions and new ways of thinking. It requires creativity to spawn the ideas and risk taking to push the ideas to innovative results.

A company will no longer survive by staying in its present state. Dr. Edward de Bono, creativity educator, says, "As competition intensifies, so does the need for creative thinking. It is no longer enough to do the same thing better. It is no longer enough to be efficient and solve problems. Far more is needed. Business needs creativity both on the strategic level and on the front line to make the shift that competitive business demands—from administration to true entrepreneurship."

Companies must become more competitive. How? To increase the competitive advantage, companies can decrease costs, increase quality, increase speed or master innovation. The changes implemented by most companies address the first three, but not usually the last. In addition, most companies are experiencing less than half the potential of the first three if the changed workplace does not encourage creativity and reward risk.

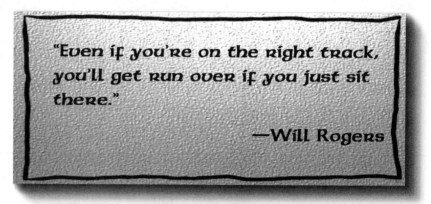

"Even if you're on the right track, you'll get run over if you just sit there."

—Will Rogers

This makes creativity imperative to ensure that corporations do more than just survive—that they thrive.

How Did Creativity Begin?

Corporate creativity had its start in the early 1950s when psychologists studying imagination, concluded that creativity could be learned and fostered. Soon after, Alex Osborn, father of brainstorming, formed the Creative Education Foundation (a clearinghouse for creativity information), started publishing the *Journal of Creative Behavior* and established the Creative Problem Solving Institute to teach executive creative problem solving. It is this last endeavor, that set the stage for how corporations would implement creativity.

Today articles about creativity appear in every business magazine and industry journal: *Fortune, Business Week, Success, Harvard Business Review, Training and Development*. Most business schools offer creativity courses. And *Training Magazine* reported in its October, 1994 issue that 44% of the 1,119 companies (100 employees or more) responding to its training survey provide creativity training.

Establishing a Creative Climate

But creativity is such a personal thing! Individuals are creative, not corporations! It's true. A corporation may be seen as a creative entity because it fosters creativity in its people. Generally a creative organization like 3M, Hallmark, Frito-Lay or Texas Instruments has created a climate that supports creative thinking. This climate would be:

Open-minded

O It encourages flexibility and creativity. It probably allows employees to experiment with using creative approaches and techniques. Creative efforts are included in the budget.

Perceptive

P The company sees things from the employees' viewpoint. There is an assurance that the work is rewarding both in a professional and personal way. A participative atmosphere is encouraged by asking for and acting upon employees' input.

Equal

E People are respected for the diversity each brings. Leadership techniques and styles are individualized to fit the needs of each employee. Employees' ideas are implemented well.

Nurturing

N Free expression of ideas are stimulated. Employees are provided with knowledge through speakers, libraries, training and other learning opportunities that provide input for creativity. Regeneration needs are accommodated through paid time off and sabbaticals.

Encouraging

E Employees are encouraged to find creative, different answers. Not only are creative efforts rewarded and reinforced, but time is built in to be creative. Freedom and opportunity for self-expression exist.

Descriptive

D Communication is very good. Clear objectives and specific feedback are basic to everything the organization does. Employees have frequent direct customer contact. A balance between structure and opportunity for creative expression exists.

You can see then that the typical approach to management, one of control (the project must be done correctly, by the book, on time, and within budget) will most likely stifle creativity. The comments that prevent creative ideas from surfacing have been coined as "killer phrases" by Dr. Sidney J. Parnes. You've heard them: "we've never done it that way before," "it's not in the budget," "it's not our policy." Doing things by the book creates an efficient organization, but certainly not an innovative one.

"Creativity is being demanded of managers, not just in the context of what they do but in the process of how they get it done," says John Kao, Ph.D., an associate professor at Harvard Business School, who teaches a course called *Entrepreneurship, Creativity and Organization*. Today, managers must do more than just develop a new product or improve efficiency. They must also be creative in how they get people to work together in teams and how they handle the human issues in organizations. They must create a climate where creativity and risk taking are stimulated and rewarded and mistakes are viewed as a part of life.

Management must work hard at creating a climate that is conducive to creativity, that exhibits the six qualities previously mentioned. With that kind of environment, individual creativity can flourish.

Will I Know It When I See It?

Defining creativity isn't easy, even for the experts.

Webster's New Collegiate Dictionary defines creativity as "the ability to create," and create as "to bring into existence; to produce or bring about by a course of action; to produce through imaginative skill; to make or bring into existence something new."

Our favorite definition is Mike Vance's (the Disney Corporation) "creativity is the making of the new and the rearranging of the old."

Most creativity experts refuse to nail down one specific definition— and rightly so. After all, how creative would creativity be if you could define it only one way?

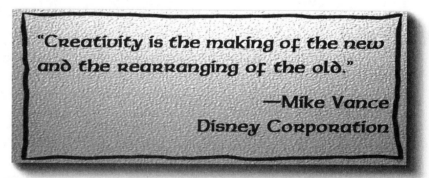

"Creativity is the making of the new and the rearranging of the old."

—Mike Vance
Disney Corporation

But one thing the experts do agree on is that creative skills can be developed, techniques can be taught and an individual's creativity can be enhanced with practice. E. Paul Torrance, J.P. Guilford and Alex Osborn all agree (and frequently demonstrate) that creativity is a skill that can be learned and honed.

Others draw a fine line distinction and say that creativity cannot be "taught." Since we are already creative, we can assist individuals to rediscover what it is to be creative. The objective is to help them unlearn the things that may keep them from being creative.

The Brain

The brain, 500 million years in the making, is the most magnificent organ in your body. It resembles a three-pound gray jellied walnut. But what that walnut can do! It has the capacity to take in, process, and program more than 600 memories each second for 85 years.

That's 36,000 each minute. . .

2,160,000 each hour. . .

and over 51,840,000 every day of your life!

The sad news is this remarkable part of your body—a muscle which thrives on exercise—is sorely underutilized. It's there to serve you 24 hours a day, yet we use a fraction of the billions of brain cells available to us. At one time it was believed that people used 10% of their brain's capacity. Scientists now believe that Einstein may have been the only human to ever approach that high of a percent. The rest of us use 2–3% of our brains.

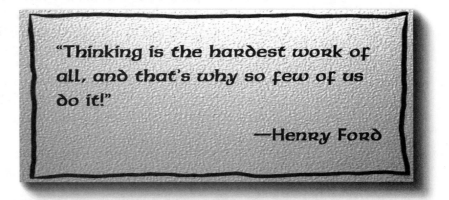

"Thinking is the hardest work of all, and that's why so few of us do it!"

—Henry Ford

So what's the rest there for? That's an unanswered question. But one thing's for sure. There is plenty of room within your cranium to expand to more creative thinking! Wake up the creative genius inside and turn more of your brain power to your advantage.

The creative thought process is based upon the idea that your brain has the ability to create an infinite number of ideas, combinations and relationships. Like a kaleidoscope, your brain can form, reform and reform again multiple patterns. These patterns and combinations create the new relationships we call "ideas."

To solve most of life's problems we usually require both inductive and deductive reasoning; creative and logical thought processes. Can your brain do all of that at the same time?

Right-Brain/Left-Brain

Right-brain, left-brain, half-brained, lame brained or whole brain. Is there actually a difference between your right brain and your left brain?

There has been much talk about "left-brain and right-brain theory." It is true that the cortex of the cerebrum's left hemisphere assumes responsibility for analytical functions and the cortex for the cerebrum's right hemisphere assumes responsibility for the imaginative functions. But it isn't that black and white. The two hemispheres are more similar than different and almost every mental process requires that they work together. Therefore, keep in mind that these are just labels, terms, and that there are no separate compartments in our brains that store or process information that simplistically.

Regions are differentiated in the brain, but the activities are integrated. In other words, the whole is greater than the sum of its parts. When you sit down to read your favorite fiction book, your left-brain is translating the written words and providing meaning, while at the same time, your right-brain is decoding the information to form pictures in your mind, understanding the metaphors, appreciating the humor and providing your feelings for the emotional content. As you can see reading a book just wouldn't be the same without both sides of your brain!

Instead, we need to understand that there are two ways of thinking that can be called left-brain thinking and right-brain thinking. We cannot do both types of thinking at the same time, and we shift from one side to the other constantly. And in many people one side is more active than the other. The most successful people are those who can easily shift from one thinking style to the other.

So of course, the best of both worlds is to use both sides of your brain. Many examples exist proving that using your right-brain for left-brained tasks is advantageous, to say nothing of lucrative.

Ibuka, honorary chairman of Sony, took a failed project—a miniature tape recorder—changed its functions and combined it with headphones to create the Walkman radio. The Jacuzzi brothers invented a whirlpool bath for a cousin who had arthritis. Fifteen years later Roy Jacuzzi sold it as a luxury bath product and made millions. In each case, problems became opportunities. In each case, right-brained thinking solved a left-brained problem.

Let's focus on this thing called creativity. If Einstein, one of the smartest people who ever lived, thought that imagination was more important than knowledge, it would stand to reason (from our left-brain thinking) that we ought to spend some time determining how to be more creative.

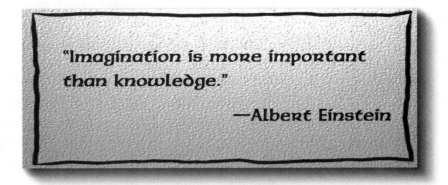

"Imagination is more important than knowledge."

—Albert Einstein

How Does One Become Creative?

An imperative first step is to believe that you have the ability to be more creative. Once you have jumped that hurdle, you are now open to investigate hundreds of tools and techniques, some with formidable names like "morphological analysis" and "nominal group technique", and others with curiosity provoking names like "squeeze and stretch" and "ask what if?"

The idea of creativity tools started when advertising executive Alex Osborn popularized brainstorming as a method for generating ideas. Since that time many techniques have spun off as methods and tools to encourage and enhance creative thinking. This sourcebook, for example, offers ten techniques whose first letters spell the word CREATIVITY (Compare and Combine; Risk Taking; Expand and Shrink; Ask What's Good? And What If?; Transform Your Viewpoint; In Another Sequence; Visit Other Places; Incubate; Trigger Concepts; and Youth's Advantage).

All of these techniques, like most creative techniques, fall into one of four strategies:

1. **Visualization**

    Seeing the preferred future, seeing the ideal.

2. **Exploration**

    Using metaphors, analogies or symbols to question assumptions and to jolt our paradigms.

3. **Combination**

    Bringing various elements together in different ways.

4. **Modification**

    Improvising, adapting, adjusting what you already have.

Each of these uses the basic guidelines of brainstorming to create new ideas. How does each differ? Let's say that you have a project that's due at work and you need to be innovative in your approach.

Visualization

If you used visualization you would consider what it would be like if you were already successful in completing it. What would you hear? What would your boss be saying? What would your customers be saying? What would you see? What would the project look like? What form would it take? What would you be feeling? What would give you those feelings?

Explorations

If you used explorations you would develop several analogies or metaphors and make comparisons, then ask yourself what these comparisons mean, what similarities there are or what differences exist. So if you compare your project with baking bread, for example, what similarities exist? Both require the right ingredients to be successful, both require time to rise. What differences? Bread can be baked by one person, the project will require more input. Now what does this tell you? Perhaps it will lead you to realize you need to have more access to a word processor, that you need to put a time line together or that you need to schedule interviews with colleagues.

Combinations

If you used combinations you might combine your project with something related or unrelated. Combining it with another task that you already have might make you realize that some of the same customers will be involved and you might be able to double up on some of your discussions with them. An unrelated combination might be to imagine combining it with a party to identify any overlaps. For example, you might want to think about how the project could be more fun. Bill Bowerman used the unlikely combination of rubber and a waffle iron and invented the Nike® shoe sole.

Modifications

If you used modifications you might go back to past projects to see how your approach could be modified in this one. Or you might ask other people about their projects and then modify your approach to what they tell you.

Within each of these strategies are many techniques. You need to worry less about which technique to use, than just using one. Each is created to jolt you out of your everyday thinking and move you to think differently—outside your box. There is no one technique or perfect approach to increasing creativity. You will have a preference. Eventually you will begin to recall what worked best for you.

Often we go through the day on automatic pilot, allowing our habits to rule the day, hoping for the predictable and avoiding surprises. This can be good because we can become efficient and effective. The drawback, however, is that our expectation of how "things should be" replaces how "things could be." And this prevents us from seeing bigger, better, wiser, wider.

These techniques will light a new spark that may ignite a blaze of creativity, and the world may never look the same again.

What Good Will Creative Thinking Do for Me?

Aha! The old what's-in-it-for-me question. There are many positive, creative actions that you can take. Creativity can benefit you on the job and at home.

How about making your job easier? Or making yourself more valuable to the company you work for? Look around. What could be improved?

- Communication?
- Processes?
- Service?
- Products?
- Teamwork?
- Planning?
- What do customers want that they don't have?
- What could be done cheaper?
- Faster?
- Better?
- What changes do you see coming in the future?

What about making your leisure time more pleasant? How could you mow that lawn faster? Or not at all? How can you take a vacation that pleases everyone in the family? How could you stretch your pay check to go farther? How can you make mealtime a pleasant experience for everyone? How could you make your hobby earn money? How could you simplify your schedule?

In addition to tangible benefits, you will find that tapping into your creative energy can be fun and add a positive outlook to everything you do. You will find yourself using your imagination to solve day-to-day problems because you are open to more and varied solutions. You will most likely eliminate boredom, increase your self-confidence and increase satisfaction in your personal relationships. And, in general, probably enjoy life more. Sound too good to be true? Try it.

How Do I Use Creativity?

First, recognize that you have an unbelievable resource in your head—a fortune in information. Once you realize that, you will be more alert to tap into it daily.

Look for ideas

Second, look for ideas: ideas that solve problems, help others, make your life easier, improve your work, improve the environment, help the company you work for. Develop a curiosity about people, places, things. Visit many places: local factories, ethnic stores, the library, other cities, other states, other countries. Talk with others from different professions, places, walks of life. Trust your intuition and pay attention to your dreams.

Build your idea sources

Continue to build your idea sources. Read many types of books and magazines. Ask questions that develop your mind: Why? What if? How? Ask questions and truly listen and learn from the answers. Read books about creativity. Start with *Whack on the Side of the Head* by Roger von Oech.

Capture these ideas

Third, capture these ideas. You need to write them down or they may be lost. In addition, having them available to read means that they may trigger other ideas. List your goals in life, parts of solutions to problems, inventions that haven't been created, seemingly silly ideas, imagined family situations.

Use your ideas

Finally, use your ideas. Certainly not all of them. But a few at first, more later. Aim high. Shoot for the moon, and even if you miss, you'll end up in the stars somewhere. Think positively. Go for the best. Expect the best. You get out of life exactly what you put into it.

> "A person who never made a mistake never tried anything new."
>
> —Albert Einstein

"But this sounds risky!" you say. Success doesn't necessarily breed success. Failure breeds success. Are you aware that Babe Ruth struck out 1330 times and in between he hit 714 home runs? When asked about all his failures in trying to make a light bulb, Edison replied that he was actually successful in knowing 1800 ways not to make a light bulb.

Do you consider a good day of skiing one in which you did not fall down? Not falling is not learning. Author Tom Peters encourages us to "fail faster." Not being creative and taking risks is not moving forward. Not moving forward means falling behind.

Be creative. Take risks.

But I'm Not A Creative Person!

Unfortunately many people put creativity on a pedestal and think that if they can't do what Edison, Shakespeare or Michelangelo did, they aren't creative.

But what about the employee who finds a faster way to deliver the mail or a better way to satisfy a customer? What about the trainer who designs a new activity or uses a new training technique? What about the parent who finds a creative way to budget the family's limited resources or creates a theme party for a child or designs an original knit sweater? Or the child who invents a new game or creates a new language? These are all creative actions.

Probably the biggest barrier to creativity is our self-imposed limitations, "I do not believe I am creative, therefore, I'm not."

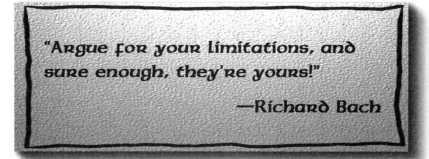

"Argue for your limitations, and sure enough, they're yours!"

—Richard Bach

The key to appreciating that we are all creative is to accept the premise that creativity is a continuum. It does not belong exclusively to the artists, authors and inventors of the world. Of course most of us will never write like Shakespeare or paint like Michelangelo or invent like Edison. That doesn't mean you aren't creative.

We are all on the creativity continuum. To move farther along that continuum, you must first accept that you are creative, and second that you can increase your creative potential.

The problem with this is that many people have told themselves for so long (all their lives) that they aren't creative, their brain believes it, and it will be difficult to break out of that personal paradigm. Difficult, but not impossible. Individuals need to have success at being creative. They need to be reinforced for being creative. They need to plant new seeds in their brains by sending messages that say, "I am creative."

Imagine what might have happened if the following people believed that they could not succeed because of messages they had been given:

- Thomas Edison was expelled from school at the age of ten, when his mother was told that his brain was addled.

- Grandma Moses was told she was too old to begin painting.

- Louis Pasteur was evaluated as a "mediocre" chemistry student.

- Walt Disney was told he had no talent as a child.

- Winston Churchill failed sixth grade and was told he was "dull."

As a trainer, your responsibility is to provide participants with a message that moves them down the creativity continuum. If you can get them to the point where they eliminate the blocks to their own creativity you will open the door to new ideas for them. Removing the box that they put themselves in will allow creativity to flow.

What Should a Creativity Workshop Look Like? Feel Like? Taste Like?

1. First of all it should be fun! Teaching techniques without making them fun will result in less than 50% success. A very important part of creativity involves helping people get outside their box. Creativity requires that certain childlike mental operations be present for maximum success. These include playfulness, wishfulness, spontaneity, stimulation, pretending, daydreaming and free-association of ideas. Creating this climate begins with fun. And fun suggests laughing, toys, crayons, talking, games, pictures, color. . . , be creative!

2. Second, it should be stimulating. This may mean considering what you can do to stimulate all the senses: sight—with posters, mobiles, displays; sound—with music, musical instruments, silence; smell—with scent bottles, scratch and sniff books; touch—with fabric swatches, Koosh Balls, Play-Doh; and taste with unique break snacks (vegetable juice and crackers), unusual food (star fruit or Pop Rocks), kids' edibles (bubble gum or Cracker Jacks).

3. Third, the content should focus on three things. First, helping people recognize and get out of their boxes—the blocks that inhibit creative expression. It should also introduce a number of techniques that can be implemented by individuals. And last, if you are presenting your workshops to a corporate audience, it is also useful to include something that addresses the organization, its creative focus and the participants' responsibility in encouraging creativity in the workplace.

4. Fourth, the information should be transferable back to the workplace. Creativity already has a reputation of being uncontrollable, unpredictable and playful. Certainly none of these are words used to describe the most successful Fortune 500 companies. So, it behooves you as a trainer to ensure that the techniques learned are presented in a fun way that taps into each participant's right brain, but that the outcomes are also practically applicable.

When asked about creativity, many managers still say that creativity is okay, but they don't want their people sitting around being creative, they want them answering the phone or fixing the gasket or stocking the shelves. If you then ask if they would like them figuring out how to answer the phone promptly, repair the gasket for good or stock the shelves faster, they say, "of course!" The key to transferability is applicability.

5. And finally, it should help participants tap into their own creative ability. Everyone leaving the workshop should "feel" more creative, more certain that they are creative and can use the techniques to which they were exposed. That may mean a healthy dose of positive thinking.

You will find that the workshops in this sourcebook meet all of these criteria.

As a trainer, this could quite possibly be the most exciting workshop you've ever conducted.

Enjoy yourself, get a little crazy and. . . be creative!

Chapter Two:

Workshop Preparation

Welcome to the colorful world of creativity! Your creativity and enthusiasm guarantee the success of this workshop, which is called *Widen Your Spectrum.* Your vision and attitude will allow others to shed light on their creative skills. In these workshops you may encounter a training environment that is new to you. These workshops were specifically designed to reach a little of the logical side of the brain and a lot of the creative side. They contain key experiences that impact the learners' attitudes as well as knowledge.

WHAT'S IN THIS CHAPTER?

This chapter will serve as a road map for you. It will introduce you to creativity training and how it might be unique from other training that you may conduct. It will provide an outline of what you can find in this book. And, finally, it will be a road map for you to prepare for a successful workshop.

A Word With the Facilitator. . .

Recognize that experiential learning which pushes the participants into their creative side can be uncomfortable at first. Be patient with them. This may mean waiting an unusual amount of time for volunteered responses. Wait silently; positively reinforce any attempts to respond and any risks that participants take. The handout, *Questioning Creativity?,* has been included to answer some participant questions and to help ease the uncertainty and discomfort that can occur when working with the unknown. Creativity can be a scary topic. Your participants will need all of the support and reinforcement you can offer.

Be persistent, patient and enthusiastic. Your participants will soon get into their right brains and realize how much fun creativity and the skills that support it can be!

What's So Special About Creativity Training?

Since this is a creativity training session, we have tried to practice what we are teaching. Therefore you will find creative (you may think unusual) suggestions and materials. What? You will find all of the following:

• The session begins in the dark (because we're still "in the dark" about creativity and need to see the light).

• Misspelled words (wright for right, because wrong begins with a "w." Do you need a better reason?).

• Instructions which may appear to have information missing (to encourage participants to be creative in their interpretation).

• No ground rules for the training session (because rules—self-imposed or otherwise—are some of the greatest inhibitors of creativity; and you will see participants making up their own rules throughout the sessions to fill in and make themselves feel comfortable).

• Crayons, clay and frisbees in the classroom (because creativity is easier if we get in touch with the child within us).

• Music is encouraged and unique foods are suggested (because creativity demands that we use all of our senses).

This guide provides you with suggestions and background information to help you in preparation, delivery and follow-up for the session. We suggest that you read it thoroughly before preparing your initial session. For many of the activities, you will be able to insert specific examples and information unique to your company. It is just this kind of commitment and effort that will enhance your participants' learning.

Content and materials are not the only factors in successful learning experiences. We recognize the importance of you, the person who presents this session to the learners. It is you who will *Widen Their Spectrum.*

As a trainer, you should always strive to model what you are teaching.

The Spectrum: Philosophy, Purpose, and Objectives

Throughout the session, you will be using activities, handouts and scripts that reflect the theory of light beaming through a prism to create the colors of the spectrum. In searching for a symbol that represents the actions and products of creativity, the spectrum passed the test. It is our conviction that given the right tools and training, people need no longer keep their creative talent in the dark. It is possible to *Widen Your Spectrum.*

The purpose of this session is to strengthen and enhance the creative skills of the participants so they will be able to achieve the following objectives:

- Define creativity.

- Identify their personal creativity boxes.

- Design their individualized creative environment.

- Use a variety of creativity techniques to encourage creative efforts.

- Understand the relationship between taking risks and creativity.

- Relate creativity to the company's culture and future needs.

- Encourage and support others' creative efforts.

- Target personal goals to increase their creative efforts.

- Use creativity skills learned in the session on the job.

Participants

This session is designed for the adult learner. Each organization must determine which of its employees would most benefit from the training. We suggest that you consider this creativity session as part of your management and supervisory training. We also suggest it be a voluntary session and that participants request enrollment.

No matter who attends, it is imperative that you brush-up on adult learning theory skills knowledge, since this training truly pushes participants' comfort limits.

Four adult learning theory principles that are particularly critical are these:

- Adults are people who have a good deal of first-hand experience and much to contribute to a learning situation.

- Adults learn because they want to or need to learn.

- Adults retain the most learning when they can put it to immediate use.

- Adults learn best when they feel physically and psychologically comfortable.

These workshops have been designed to easily incorporate the first three principles. The last is one to which you will want to pay special attention. The workshops are designed to push people into a different thinking mode. And, although they are designed to begin with mildly creative activities and work up to more creative activities, everyone will not move at the same rate. Be supportive of these folks.

Support Within These Two Covers

What You Will Find in This Sourcebook

Chapter 1   **Why Creativity?**

Chapter 1 provides an overview and introduction to the topic of creativity.

Chapter 2   **Workshop Preparation**

Chapter 2 includes training tips and organizational materials to help you prepare for a successful workshop.

In addition, the Subject/Reference Matrix will help you choose the workshop topics that meet your training needs.

Chapters 3, 4, and 5   **One-Day, Half-Day and One-Hour Workshops**

Chapter 3 is the one-day workshop, Chapter 4 is the half-day workshop, and Chapter 5 presents four one-hour workshops (three of these present new material). Each of these chapters provides you with an introduction that tells you what you need to prepare for the workshop, which handouts you will need, which overhead transparencies you will need, special materials required, how to set up your room, and finally, a detailed training plan with step-by-step instructions for the workshop.

Chapter 6   **Participant Handouts**

Chapter 6 provides masters of all the handout materials you will need for all of the workshops—plus three optional handouts.

Chapter 7   **Learning Activities**

Chapter 7 is a real bonus. It provides you with 23 activities that you can use. About two-thirds are activities from the workshops that have been redesigned to be self-contained and independent. One-third of them are new activities not found in the workshops. You can use these activities in many ways. You may use them specifically for teaching creativity skills, or as a part of other workshops. Creativity techniques are of course useful whether you are teaching selling skills, team building, stress management or diversity awareness.

Chapter 8   **Managing Creativity**

Chapter 8 contains masters of optional instruments you may choose to use as well as recommendations for others.

Chapter 9	**Overhead Transparencies**

Chapter 9 is where you will find the masters for your overhead transparencies plus other supplemental materials (award, group table tents).

Appendix   **Recommended Resources**

Don't forget to check the appendix. You will find supplemental workshop materials, creativity tools, a suggested reading and resource list, instruments, videos and brainstorming software, as well as how to locate these materials.

Workshop Topics

In this sourcebook, you have all the information needed to create your own creativity training programs. The following pages provide Subject/Reference matrices to help you select the topics that fit your objectives.

Procedure

To choose the topics needed for your training program, follow the steps below:

1. To locate sourcebook material on a specific topic, go to Column A and find the row that lists the topic needed.

2. Refer to the cells in that row to find page references for information and materials on the topic.

Subject/Reference Matrix

A. Topic	B. Module	C. Trainer's Notes/Scripts	D. Activity/Handouts	E. Supplies	F. Overheads/Visual Aids
Introduction	In the Dark		Questioning Creativity? (p. 136)	Flashlights / Tape deck, music	
Right-Brain/Left-Brain	In the Dark	Meet the Creative Me (p. 195)	Meet the Creative Me (p. 138)	Crayons	Group table tents (pp. 284-288)
			Right Brain/Left Brain? (p. 141)		Left Brain/Right Brain? (p. 267) / Whole Brain Thinking (p. 268)
	In the Dark	Can Creativity Be Defined? (p. 197)	Can Creativity Be Defined? (p. 139)		Dictionary (p. 265) / Making of the New (p. 266)
			Creativity Needs Assessment (p. 255)		
		Do You Know. . . ? (p. 201)	Do You Know. . . ? (p. 140)		
	In the Dark	Getting Out of the Box (pp. 206-207) / Unbox Your Creativity (pp. 208-212)	Nine Uncreative Boxes (p. 142) / Unbox Your Creativity (pp. 143-147)	Dollar bill, quarter / Crayons	Nine Uncreative Boxes (p. 270)
	(optional)	Left Brain/Right Brain Shift (p. 248)		Paper / Simple line drawings	
	(optional)	Characteristics of Creative People (p. 246)			
Energizers	In the Dark		Toy Break (pp. 68, 102)	Toy table	Discovery Consists (p. 269)
	In the Dark	Nine Uncreative Boxes (p. 142)	Out of Your Box Break (pp. 71, 107)		Opportunityisnowhere (p. 271) / Unbox Your Creativity (p. 272)
	See the Light		Idea Sparker (p. 148)		
	See the Light	Color-Blind Energizer (p. 213)	Color-Blind Engergizer (p. 213)	Idea Sparker Cards (if available)	
	(optional)	Eyedeas Energizer (p. 243)	Eyedeas (p. 190)		

Subject/Reference Matrix

A. Topic	B. Module	C. Trainer's Notes/Scripts	D. Activity/Handouts	E. Supplies	F. Overheads/Visual Aids
Energizers (cont.)	(optional)	Kid's Game Energizer (p. 245)	Kid's Game (p. 192)		
	Light Your Company's Creativity	Thumbprints Energizer (p. 235)	Thumbprints Energizer (no handout) (p. 235)	Ink pads, paper Tape deck, music	
Creative Environment		My Creative Climate (p. 214)	My Creative Climate (p. 149)		A Spectrum of Creativity Techniques (p. 273)
	Light Your Company's Creativity	Creativity Climate Survey Scoring (p. 166)	Creativity Climate Survey (p. 164) Opened Climates (p. 167)		
	Light Your Company's Creativity		The Company's Creative Past (p. 163)		The Company's Creative Past (p. 275)
	Light Your Company's Creativity	Road to Success (p. 223) Script (p. 225)	Opened Climates (p. 167)	Slides (if available) Crayons, Play-Doh	Flower (p. 281) Where Can Creativity Flourish? (p. 276)
	Light Your Company's Creativity		The Company's Creative Future (no handout) (p. 81) Killer Phrases (p. 169) Where Can Creativity Flourish? (p. 170)		Where Can Creativity Flourish? (p. 276)
	(optional)	Your Creative Style (p. 244)	Your Creative Style (p. 191)		
		Killer Phrases (p. 233)		Blank paper	
Creativity Process and Techniques	See the Light	A Spectrum of Creativity Techniques (p. 217)	Your Creative Spectrum (pp. 152-162)	Group table tents (pp. 284-288)	A Spectrum of Creativity Techniques (p. 273)
		Ten Idea-Generating Techniques (p. 219)			A Spectrum of Creativity Techniques (p. 273)
	The Creativity Process (One-Hour Workshop)	The Five R's of Creativity (p. 238)	The Five R's of Creativity (p. 187) Steps in the Creative Process (p. 188)	Crayons	The Five R's of Creativity (pp. 282-283)
A Taste of Creativity (One-Hour Workshop)		My Creative Viewpoint (p. 199)	My Creative Viewpoint (p. 179) A Taste of Creativity: Definition (p. 180)	Kid-like food Crayons, paper	Making of the New (p. 266) Dictionary (p. 265)

Subject/Reference Matrix

A. Topic	B. Module	C. Trainer's Notes/Scripts	D. Activity/Handouts	E. Supplies	F. Overheads/Visual Aids
Risk Taking	See the Light		Take a Risk to Lunch (p. 75)		
	See the Light	Take a Risk (p. 216)	Risky Business (p. 151)		Turtle Race (p. 274) Turtle Award (p. 289)
			Creativity Climate Survey (p. 164)		
	Light Your Company's Creativity	Road to Success (p. 223) Script (p. 225)			
	Light Your Company's Creativity	The Company's Creative Future (p. 81)	Killer Phrases (p. 169) Opend Climates (pp. 167-168)		
Brainstorming	Flash Your Creativity	Brainstorming Plans for Personal Creativity (p. 236)	Brainstorming (p. 171) What Can You Do? (p. 173)		Brainstorming (p. 277)
	Flash Your Creativity	Lighting Others' Creativity (p. 237)	Lighting Others' Creativity (p. 174) Reading List (p. 177)		Candle With Quote (p. 278) Creative Flashes (p. 179) Come Out of Your Shell (p. 280) Flower (p. 281)
	Getting Unstuck (One-Hour Workshop)		Brainstorming (p. 171)	Crayons Toys Colored markers Masking tape 400 index cards	
	So You Think You Have an Idea... (One-Hour Workshop)		So You Think You Have an Idea. . . (p. 181) From Here to There (p. 182) What's Next? (p. 183)	Books	
Conclusion	(optional)	Signs of Creativity (p. 250)	Creatively Yours (p. 176)	Envelope	
				Flipchart sheets Crayons Water colors Colored markers	

Navigating the Training Plans

The training plans are the heart of each of the seminar and workshop sessions. These training plans are set out in detail on a module-by-module basis, with an agenda, statement of purpose, and objectives for each module. We have attempted to make these training plans as easy to use and as complete as possible. The icons are translated on the next page and a sample page with annotations is on page 26.

1. Each section within a module has a heading that includes a statement of objectives for the section, suggested timing, and materials needed.

2. Within each section, you will find one or more major activities, each marked by an icon and a descriptive heading.

3. Additionally, you will find a number of supporting activities, each marked with an icon and explained with a suggested action.

4. Suggested actions are shown in conjunction with supporting activities, with the appropriate action verb in *UPPERCASE BOLD ITALIC*.

5. Suggested comments accompany many of the suggested actions. While these comments are fully "scripted," it is not intended that you "parrot" these remarks—but rather paraphrase the key thoughts in a way that is meaningful to you and the participants.

Understanding the Icons

Major activities

The following icons mark major activities:

 Activities that feature facilitator commentary. In these activities, you—as facilitator—present information that will be key to subsequent workshop activities.

 Activities carried out in small groups. You assign participants to small groups to complete the activity at hand. This icon is also used as a signal to listen for specific comments.

 Activities that revolve around total training group discussion. Such activities typically follow major exercises on which participants have worked individually or in groups.

 Activities to be completed on an individual basis.

Supporting activities

The following icons mark supporting activities:

 An overhead transparency is to be shown. The title of the overhead transparency is referenced in the text accompanying the icon.

 A participant handout, part or all of a learning activity, or an assessment is to be handed out.

 A question is to be asked. Wording for the question is provided, as are suggested answers when appropriate.

 A flipchart is to be used. If the flipchart is one of the "prepared flipcharts" recommended for the workshop, its title will appear in the accompanying text.

Notes

The following icons mark notes to the facilitator:

✳ Indicates a special note or suggested pre-work.

⧖ Indicates when to call time for timed exercises.

▦ Marks the end of an exercise or section.

Sample Page

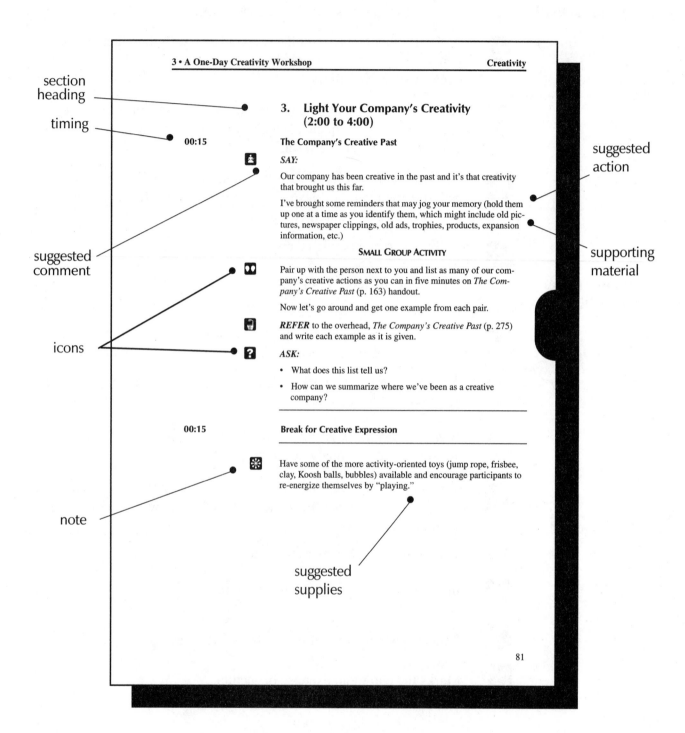

section heading

timing

suggested comment

icons

note

suggested action

supporting material

suggested supplies

Content within the sample page:

3. Light Your Company's Creativity
(2:00 to 4:00)

00:15

The Company's Creative Past

SAY:

Our company has been creative in the past and it's that creativity that brought us this far.

I've brought some reminders that may jog your memory (hold them up one at a time as you identify them, which might include old pictures, newspaper clippings, old ads, trophies, products, expansion information, etc.)

SMALL GROUP ACTIVITY

Pair up with the person next to you and list as many of our company's creative actions as you can in five minutes on *The Company's Creative Past* (p. 163) handout.

Now let's go around and get one example from each pair.

REFER to the overhead, *The Company's Creative Past* (p. 275) and write each example as it is given.

ASK:

• What does this list tell us?

• How can we summarize where we've been as a creative company?

00:15

Break for Creative Expression

Have some of the more activity-oriented toys (jump rope, frisbee, clay, Koosh balls, bubbles) available and encourage participants to re-energize themselves by "playing."

81

Becoming Familiar With the Material

First read Chapter 3 thoroughly. It will give you the full scope since it covers most of the activities in the book. As you read Chapter 3, refer to the handouts in Chapter 6 as well as the overhead transparencies in Chapter 9. This will give you a total vision of the training, from start to finish. At a later time you will want to complete all of the activities yourself.

You will notice that the training plans are complete including activity headings, timing, suggested comments and questions with potential responses. Overhead transparencies and handouts are identified when they are used.

Notice also, the icons that will guide you as you conduct the workshop. If you relate well to colors, you may choose to fill some in with colored markers as an assist to you.

Once you've completed studying Chapter 3, page through Chapter 4 to see how it differs in focus from the one-day session. Read Chapter 5, since the four one-hour workshops are different and you may wish to substitute one, or use it as a pre-workshop to generate enthusiasm.

Next, page through Chapter 7 to see the activities that are the same as those in the one-day and how they differ as activities that you can insert in other sessions. Also check out the activities that are different from those in Chapters 3, 4, and 5.

Finally, look at the instruments in Chapter 8 and the Appendix to determine if you would like to use any of these materials.

Customization Ideas

We believe that training should fit your culture. You should not try to force-fit any training into your culture. On the other hand, we know how costly it is to purchase or develop a customized training package for everything. If you want to tailor some of the pieces for your organization, we have listed several places where you might consider doing that, as well as a few tips for how.

You have probably already noticed that the workshop has a corporate focus. If you work in a volunteer organization, an association, government or something other than the corporate world, you may want to change the wording to meet your organization's needs.

Probably the easiest way to do this is to create handouts that could substitute for some of the pages in the participants' materials. The following pages could be easily tailored. You may wish to redo the entire page, or just use white typing tape to cover what you don't want (it comes in a 3/4" width) and type over it.

Cover page

Customize the cover page by adding your organization's name and logo. You may also change the name *Widen Your Spectrum* to a title your company prefers.

Handouts

Questioning Creativity?

You may replace this handout with a welcome letter or statement by your CEO or President— or perhaps a history or status report on creativity in your own organization.

Spectrum of Creativity Techniques

Almost all of these could identify actual problems your organization or the departments in the session are facing. Use an upcoming event or project on which to practice the techniques.

The Company's Creative Past

Substitute a picture of your company's buildings or logo or perhaps some graphic from its past history.

The 5 R's of Creativity

You may choose to substitute your organization's problem solving methodology for the 5 R's.

Light Your Company's Creativity

Light Your Company's Creativity could be based on the needs assessment (in Chapter 8). It could also be expanded or decreased easily. This is a good stand-alone module. You might also consider bringing your CEO or President into the session for a presentation about the importance of creativity in the company and why the company is encouraging this workshop.

If you have conducted a needs assessment, you may want to build the entire workshop around it. Therefore, you could choose several of the concerns and use them as the challenges on which to practice the creativity techniques.

In general, you could build in examples from your company, your industry or your city to personalize the creativity stories in the text. Ask other people in your organization. You are sure to get some interesting stories.

Awards

Awards are an effective way to demonstrate the importance of creativity. Once the training is completed, your company may wish to distribute an award for creative efforts to each participant. Such an award may be a published certificate of completion and/or a token representing creativity. These suggestions may get you started:

- Crystal prisms.
- Kaleidoscopes.
- Creativity books.

You're limited only by your own creativity (and budget, of course!). Your organization may want to add its logo or a creativity symbol to the award as well.

Communicating With Your Participants

Invitations to Your Workshop

Notice that the heading for this paragraph is not "workshop announcement" or "workshop confirmation" which is what you might typically expect. The word "invitation" conveys a sense of expectancy and fun. It communicates this theme and motivates your participants from the first contact. As you move through this sourcebook and become familiar with the workshops you will see why this is such a natural first step.

Lucie Barron Eggleston encourages us in an article in the May, 1995 issue of *Training and Development*, to "invite" rather than "announce" or "confirm" workshop attendance. Many of the following ideas are based on her article.

How can you make your invitation fun and motivating? Perhaps you can pique participants' interest by using a quote, like the many found throughout this book, or by asking a question: "What do dreams have to do with your next project?" or "Which uncreative box do you have yourself in?" Perhaps include a riddle or a creativity exercise.

Perhaps you could send participants a short article about creativity—make it fun! Or suggest that they bring an object to the workshop. The object could be an example of their creativity, something that makes them feel creative or something that symbolizes creativity. These objects could be used during introductions or as analogies during some of the activities.

Finally, think about the format of the invitation. Plain white paper straight off the copy machine just won't do. You could use bright colored paper, add graphics, add a cartoon, color it, add glitter, write the words in a circle, write it with crayons or even send it in the shape of a paper airplane. There should be no limit to your creativity!

Sample Invitations

YOU ∎ ARE ∎ INVITED ∎ TO

WIDEN ∎ YOUR ∎ SPECTRUM

You're invited . . .

Follow-Up

Session evaluations will be completed at the conclusion of the one-day and the half-day workshops. This information should give you information for improving the next workshop.

You will also want to keep the creative spark alive in your participants. The *Creatively Yours* action plans that the participants complete at the conclusion of the session will do just that. You will mail them back to the participants four weeks after the workshop.

There are other things you may do also. These suggestions may get your creative juices flowing:

- Hold a follow-up brown bag lunch for the participants using one of the one-hour workshops. You may choose to deliver their letter to them at that time and bring some of the reminders from the original session (e.g., crayons, bubble gum, whatever was memorable for the participants).

- Conduct a closing activity in which participants plan how they will share the information and their ideas with their bosses, their work units or even their families.

- Hold a family night in which you conduct some mini-creativity exercises, set up the toy table, and display creativity books. Use the participants to help coordinate and host the event.

- Take pictures of the participants in action at the workshop. Have a double set printed. Display one set on a bulletin board outside your office. Send the second set of photos to the participants.

- Have participants partner (buddy) and establish a time that they will meet for lunch or telephone each other to ask how they have continued to be creative.

- Have participants start a journal. Provide journals as they leave the workshop.

- Start a Creative Contributors group. Participants would meet once a week to share how they used creativity to contribute to their family, community, company or world!

- Provide a list of the creativity books in your resource library and encourage people to check them out and read them.

Preparing for a Successful Workshop

Your "To Do" List

The following checklist can be reproduced each time you present *Widen Your Spectrum*. It contains pre-training and post-training time lines.

Eight weeks before

☐ Read your sourcebook thoroughly.

☐ Reserve the training room and provide a drawing of the set-up.

☐ Identify participants.

☐ Send invitations.

☐ Determine how you will package the handouts (spiral bound, 3-ring binder, stapled, in a pocket folder) .

☐ Determine how you will add color to your overhead transpare n-cies.

☐ Have the transparencies made (if this is your first session).

☐ Order any special materials you may need for the session (crayons, clay—see the materials list) .

Six weeks before

☐ Determine if and how you will customize any of the activities for your organization.

☐ Customize your notes: add your own examples, ideas and info r-mation to the content pages; use the large left-hand margin for your notes.

☐ Complete all of the activities yourself.

☐ Begin to practice the activities using the transparencies and other props.

☐ Finalize the handouts you will use.

Four weeks before
- ☐ Order refreshments.
- ☐ Check to make sure you have all the supplies.
- ☐ Fill a box with your toys.
- ☐ Have the handouts printed and bound.
- ☐ Gather resources for the *Company's Creative Past* activity.
- ☐ Continue to practice the activities.

Two weeks before
- ☐ Check the printed handouts.
- ☐ Continue to practice the activities.

One week before
- ☐ Prepare your pre-printed flipcharts.
- ☐ Check the session-at-a-glance and add things that would help you stay organized.
- ☐ Continue to practice the activities.

One day before
- ☐ Check your room, equipment and materials lists at the end of this section.
- ☐ Set up the room.
- ☐ Prepare your flipcharts.
- ☐ Double check that your equipment works.
- ☐ Double check that you have all your materials.
- ☐ Put your notes and transparencies in place.
- ☐ Get a good night's sleep.

One day after
- ☐ Analyze the evaluations; identify areas to be modified.

Four weeks after
- ☐ Send the *Creatively Yours* follow-up.

Your Room Set-Up

Select a room that enhances the workshop. You'll want one that is pleasant as well as practical. The maximum number of people recommended for any of the workshops is 20. So room size shouldn't be a problem. The best table arrangement is a U-shape. Remember, however, that you will also want a toy table and perhaps space for a refreshment table. You will want a table in the front of the room on which to place your overhead projector.

In addition to the right size, select a room that:

- Does not have any posts or barriers that may block the view.

- Has wall space for posting flipchart paper.

- Has sufficient lighting, ventilation and temperature controls.

- Has restrooms, telephones and refreshments located nearby

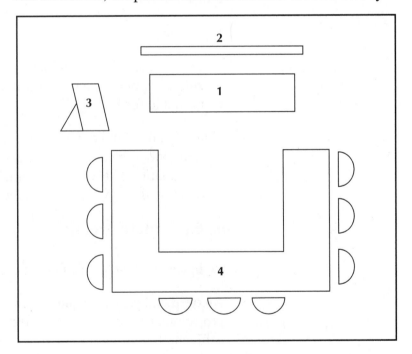

Legend

1. Facilitator's table

2. Projection screen

3. Flipchart stand

4. Participant tables and seating

We strongly recommend that you set up your room the evening before the session. This gives you time to locate anything that may have been forgotten. It also prevents that last minute rush to get everything done. What can you set up?

- Place tables and chairs in a U-shape.

- Place participant material, flashlight and a table tent at each participant's place.

- Place colored Mr. Sketch markers on the tables, at least one for every other participant.

- Place crayons, Play-Doh and other creative materials on the table.

- Organize your toy table.

- Set up the overhead transparency projector and screen and tape down the cord.

- Focus the projector.

- Place your sourcebook, trainer's notes, transparencies, markers and other supplies where they will be convenient and comfortable for you.

- A nice "to do" but not necessary, is to display some books or journals about creativity that your organization's library may have available. This often encourages participants to continue learning on their own following the session.

Your Equipment Needs

You will need to have the following equipment for this session:

- An overhead projector and screen. (If you have a choice of projectors, try them out. Many older models do not cast sufficient light to highlight your colored transparencies.)

- Place your overhead projector on a table (as opposed to a projection cart) so that you have room for supplies, your transparencies, sourcebook, a glass of water or anything else you may need.

- A flipchart stand with a full pad of paper.

- Have an extension cord, extra projector bulb and an adaptor plug on hand—just in case.

Handouts and Overhead Transparencies

The *ASTD Trainer's Sourcebook* provides you with all the participant handouts and overhead transparency masters you will need for the sessions. Of course, you are always encouraged to tailor, customize or develop your own. Masters for the handouts are in Chapter 6. Masters for the overhead transparencies are in Chapter 9.

What do you need to do about handouts?

- Read the introduction to Chapter 6, where the handouts are located, for more details.

- Review all of the handouts before you facilitate the workshop, completing the activities so that you know how you would respond to the requests you will make of the participants.

- Once you know which workshop you're going to conduct, copy the appropriate handouts. Those you will need will be listed at the beginning of each workshop chapter.

- You need to decide how to bind these materials. Suggestions can be found in Chapter 6.

What do you need to do about overhead transparencies?

- Read the introduction to Chapter 9, where the overhead transparencies are located, for more details.

- Once you decide which workshop to conduct, copy the masters onto acetates. We strongly recommend that you "make them colorful" in some way. Suggestions are given in Chapter 9.

- For a professional appearance, be sure to put them into transparency frames before you use them.

- Always practice with your transparencies before you use them.

Materials and Supplies

Use this checklist to ensure that you have the correct materials and supplies available. Note that each workshop provides a list of everything you will need for that particular workshop. This list gives you an overview of the kinds of things you will need.

☐ Your facilitator notes.

☐ Participant handouts (listed at the beginning of each workshop).

☐ Table tents.

☐ "Flash Your Creativity" flashlights (penlight flashlights—one per participant).

☐ Transparency set (listed at the beginning of each workshop).

☐ Transparency markers.

☐ Mr. Sketch markers (at least one box of mixed colors) .

☐ Audio cassette player, creativity-sparking musical tapes .

☐ Box of crayons for every 3 or 4 participants.

☐ Small can of Play-Doh for every 3 or 4 participants.

☐ A crisp one dollar bill and a quarter.

☐ Materials needed to stimulate senses as defined by you.

☐ Toys of your choice from your toy box.

☐ Idea Sparker Cards (p. 291).

☐ Samples of kid's fun food (e.g., Pop Rocks, Cracker Jacks, Bazooka bubble gum).

☐ Group table tents (pp. 284-288).

☐ Turtle Awards (p. 289).

☐ Ink pads.

☐ Road to Success Script (p. 225) and slides (p. 292).

☐ Masking tape.

☐ Blank envelopes, one per participant.

☐ Materials for optional activities of your choice :

_____

_____

_____

_____

Suggestions for Your "Toy Table"

- ☐ Coloring books.
- ☐ Play-Doh.
- ☐ Jump rope.
- ☐ Soft Frisbee.
- ☐ Kaleidoscopes.
- ☐ Yo-yo.
- ☐ Pickup sticks.
- ☐ Jacks.
- ☐ Nerf ball.
- ☐ Clay.
- ☐ Koosh ball.
- ☐ Puzzles.
- ☐ Paddle ball.
- ☐ Marbles.
- ☐ Juggling items.
- ☐ Prisms.
- ☐ Harmonica.
- ☐ Bubbles.
- ☐ Colored chalk.
- ☐ Kazoo.
- ☐ Crayons.

    (Especially the neon, glitter, metallic swirl, scented, fluorescent or any others that are new on the market.)

Your Sense Energizers

Creativity is enhanced by stimuli to the brain. You may wish to provide some of these stimuli. The types of stimuli that "spark" each individual's creativity will vary from person to person. Therefore, it is important that you provide stimuli for all five of the senses. For each module, devise situations that provide these experiences. Many are designed for you.

Use the following suggestions for the kinds of experiences you could offer. Determine what is appropriate and use your creativity to modify these to meet your participants' needs. Decide what's acceptable to most people, and push it one step farther to the right. However, overuse of these can create negative responses in some people. Only you are able to assess your participants. Be aware that total abstinence from such stimuli will cheat your participants of valuable learning. Choose wisely; adapt and create.

Sight

Add color (flowers, wall graphics, aquarium, balloons).

- Display artwork (paintings, photographs, sculpture, mobiles, posters, collages).

- Consider special effects (strobe lights, laser lights, bubble machines).

- Prepare displays (props, resources, seashell collection).

Hearing

Use audio tapes for background sounds during activities (instrumental, new age music, environmental sounds).

- Have a small electronic keyboard available during breaks.

- Play tapes during the breaks.

- Have simple "sound makers" available (kazoo, harmonica, bells, tambourine, etc.).

Touch

Have materials available that feel rough, smooth, hot, cold.

- Soft clay is ideal for participants to handle during the session.

- Provide fabric swatches at the participants' tables.

- Provide early childhood experiences (sand table, crayons, finger paint).

Taste

Take time to plan a unique snack for break. If you always have donuts and coffee, offer crackers and cheese and vegetable juice.

Have food available during parts of the session (lemon drops, mini crackers, popcorn, bubble gum, Cracker Jacks, Pop Rocks).

Smell

Put samples of different smells into new pill bottles using such smells as: clove, lemon, mint, onion, motor oil, etc. Place these around the room and have participants sniff these and record the emotions/thoughts these different smells evoke within them.

- Use room fragrance machines that place odors into the air. Request participant reaction to these.

- Use scented candles (e.g., vanilla, cinnamon, floral, spice), however, check into your company's safety rules first.

Facilitator Tips

Prepare for the Best Session Ever!

- Know what's in your sourcebook.

- Read and practice with your notes. You should be very familiar with them.

- Practice your materials outloud.

- Practice with the visuals.

- Have a plan for your flipcharts. Generally the prepared charts should be at your dominant side and the blank flipchart at your non-dominant side. Both should be at a slight angle toward your audience. This allows you to write on the blank flipchart while still seeing three-quarters of the group.

- Write your own transitions that relate to you, your organization, your participants.

- Add your personal touch with your own examples or stories.

- Personalize the notes by highlighting words, adding notes in the margin or underlining key phrases.

- Fine-tune your facilitation

Create a Safe Learning Environment

- Your main objective is to create and maintain a safe learning environment. The content and activities may be challenging for some.

- Open with energy and enthusiasm.

- Maintain good eye contact with participants. You need to connect with them. You need to read them. Do they understand? Are they lost? Do they need a break?

- Be very careful to not talk over their heads with jargon or turn them off with trainer/facilitator talk.

- Be flexible. Given a natural, teachable moment versus waiting until the topic is planned in the schedule, take the first whenever you can. You will seem more responsive to their needs and can shorten that part of the session later.

- Be open and "others-oriented."

- Be sure to recognize and reinforce participation.

Acquire and Use Excellent Delivery Skills

- Visuals are imperative for learning. They get the point across faster. They illustrate the point clearer. They increase retention. The visuals included in the training plans should be considered the minimum. Add to them where you wish.

- On the other hand, don't speak to the visual. Talk to the participants.

- Use a pointer (translucent stir stick, appetizer pick or pencil) or the revealing technique (a heavy piece of paper placed under the transparency so that you can see the next item before revealing it to the participants).

- Remind participants to turn the pages with you.

- Do not apologize for the content. Some very simple concept to you may be very new and important to another.

- Perfect your transitions. This is what makes a complex session flow and make sense to participants.

Facilitate Dynamite Activities!

- Arrange participants in small groups. Provide the activity instructions after they settle into their groups.

- Be sure to circulate during the activities. You will be needed to clarify instructions or assist with learning new skills.

- Watch the time on activities closely. A lot is packed into the workshops so you won't want to fall behind.

- Give time limit warnings before the time to complete an activity is up: "Wrap up in one minute." "You're about half way through your time." "You should be in the last half of the exercise now." "You have about five minutes left."

- If it is somewhat of an open-ended activity check with the groups individually on their progress. "How much longer will you need?" "The other groups say they need five more minutes. Will you be finished by then?"

- Though making sure you have time for everything is important, you still need to make sure you schedule enough breaks. There's no reason to force the group through an activity if no one's listening or participating!

- Process all activities. Prepare and ask questions that summarize the key learnings, that identify feelings and thoughts, that highlight alternative behaviors and that bring the skills back to the real world.

Communicate, Communicate, Communicate!

- Be specific.

- But at the same time be personable, creative and interested.

- Watch your body language.

- If you get a difficult question, turn it back to the participants. Remember, "I don't know, but I will find out and let you know by _____," is an acceptable response.

- Use a variety of questioning techniques to encourage participation: open, closed, leading. Think about the purpose of the question:

    - Are you looking for a correct answer?

    - Are you trying to create a discussion?

    - Are you trying to stimulate thinking?

    - Are you trying to tap a known expert in the group?

    - Are you trying to increase participation from a specific individual?

    - Are you trying to get the participants to take ownership?

    - Are you trying to bring out opposing points of view?

    - Are you trying to balance participation?

    - Are you trying to clarify a comment or question?

    - Are you trying to get them back on track?

    - Are you asking them to take the information the next step to apply it to their own situation?

    - (You need to determine the purpose of the question to ensure that you will get the response you want.)

- And finally, but most importantly, be an excellent listener. Listen for both the content and the intent of the statement or question. You will want to understand the speaker's perspective. Of all the skills to model as the facilitator, this is the most important.

Continue to Improve

As a facilitator, you should focus on continuously improving your own skills and processes.

How can you continue to improve your skills as a facilitator? Make a commitment to improve your own skills by trying some of these:

- View another facilitator to obtain new techniques.

- Work with a partner and provide feedback to each other.

- Provide demonstrations for specific activities to other facilitators to obtain feedback.

- Enroll in a train-the-trainer, preferably one in which you are videotaped, and obtain feedback on your style.

- Read. There are many good books and newsletters about facilitator techniques.

- Join the American Society for Training and Development (ASTD) and mingle with other professionals.

- Subscribe to one of the journals: *Training and Development* from ASTD or *Training Magazine* from Lakewood Publications.

How can you continue to improve the creativity workshops?

- Pay attention to what your customers (participants) tell you on the evaluation. Make appropriate changes.

- Be aware of your customers' (participants') changing needs. Adapt the material and the workshops to them.

- Trial run new activities with other facilitators before you conduct them in a workshop.

- If you work in a team of facilitators, share new ideas, stories and examples with each other.

- Provide follow-up several weeks after the session to learn what concepts they are using, what they would have liked you to spend more or less time on, what they still need.

- Read the books identified in the appendix as a resource to keep you fresh and give you new ideas.

Name Tent

widen your spectrum

widen your spectrum

Participant Name

Participant Name

Participant Roster

Trainer(s): _____

Date: _____   **Time**: _____

Location: _____

_____

	Participant Name	**Extension**	**Department**
1.	_____	_____	_____
2.	_____	_____	_____
3.	_____	_____	_____
4.	_____	_____	_____
5.	_____	_____	_____
6.	_____	_____	_____
7.	_____	_____	_____
8.	_____	_____	_____
9.	_____	_____	_____
10.	_____	_____	_____
11.	_____	_____	_____
12.	_____	_____	_____
13.	_____	_____	_____
14.	_____	_____	_____
15.	_____	_____	_____
16.	_____	_____	_____
17.	_____	_____	_____
18.	_____	_____	_____
19.	_____	_____	_____
20.	_____	_____	_____

Workshop Certificate

Chapter Three:

One-Day Creativity Workshop

This chapter of *CREATIVITY: The ASTD Trainer's Sourcebook* contains the training plan for your one-day creativity workshop. You may use it exactly as it is. It has been conducted dozens of times, so you can be assured that it works. Or you may tailor it to meet your needs. Chapter 2 provides tailoring suggestions.

This one-day workshop has been developed for any group of people who want to enhance their creative abilities. It has a corporate focus so if you are not using it in a company, you may want to make some changes.

WHAT'S IN THIS CHAPTER?

This chapter's main focus is to prepare you for the one-day workshop. In it you will find:

- Purpose and objectives of the workshop.
- Facilitator preparation.
- Workshop agenda.
- Detailed one-day training design.

We recommend that you read Chapter 2 because this chapter provides only the details that are unique to the one-day design. If you have not yet done so, read Chapter 2 for a detailed description about how to prepare for facilitating a creativity session. It also provides you with suggestions for how to use the sourcebook effectively.

Workshop Purpose and Objectives

The overall purpose of this creativity workshop is to introduce participants to the concept of creativity. The one-day design provides an opportunity for participants to get in touch with their personal beliefs about creativity and to practice creativity-enhancing techniques. Participants also examine their company's past, present and future with regard to creativity.

As a result of this one-day session participants will be able to:

- Define creativity.

- Identify their personal creativity boxes.

- Design their individualized creative environment.

- Use a variety of creativity techniques to encourage creative efforts.

- Understand the relationship of taking risks and creativity.

- Relate creativity to the company's culture and future needs.

- Encourage and support others' creative efforts.

- Target personal goals to increase their creative efforts.

- Use creativity skills learned in the session on the job.

Facilitator Preparation

Recommended Number of Participants

Due to the high concentration of information and the need for hands-on skill practice, we recommend limiting the workshop to 16–20 people.

Room Set-Up Suggestions

Ideally, the training room should have no windows. At the minimum, you must be able to darken the room for the opening activity. Read the Trainer's Notes and add your own comments and ideas.

- Have training room arranged for small group work. (We suggest round tables or U-shape configuration.)

- Place a flashlight, set of participant materials and table tent at each participant's place.

- Set boxes of crayons and small cans of Play-Doh (about one of each for every three participants) on the training tables, spread out so that all participants can reach one or the other easily.

- Set up a toy table with toys of your choice and other sensory stimulating materials.

- We suggest that you play "mood" music quietly as participants enter the training room.

Workshop Agenda

1. In the Dark	Minutes 3 hrs.	Start / Stop 8:00 / 11:00	Actual Start / Stop
Introduction	20	8:00 / 8:20	_____ / _____
Meet the Creative Me	20	8:20 / 8:40	_____ / _____
Objectives	5	8:40 / 8:45	_____ / _____
Can Creativity Be Defined?	20	8:45 / 9:05	_____ / _____
Do You Know. . . ?	20	9:05 / 9:25	_____ / _____
Right-Brain/Left-Brain?	10	9:25 / 9:35	_____ / _____
Toy Break	15	9:35 / 9:50	_____ / _____
Nine Uncreative Boxes	15	9:50 / 10:05	_____ / _____
Unbox Your Creativity	45	10:05 / 10:50	_____ / _____
Out of Your Box Break	10	10:50 / 11:00	_____ / _____

2. See the Light	Minutes 3 hrs.	Start / Stop 11:00 / 2:00	Actual Start / Stop
Idea Sparker	10	11:00 / 11:10	_____ / _____
My Creative Climate	15	11:10 / 11:25	_____ / _____
A Spectrum of Creativity Techniques	35	11:25 / 12:00	_____ / _____
Lunch: Take a Risk to Lunch	60	12:00 / 1:00	_____ / _____
Share Risky Business	10	1:00 / 1:10	_____ / _____
Your Creative Spectrum Practice	50	1:10 / 2:00	_____ / _____

3. Light Your Company's Creativity	Minutes 2 hrs.	Start / Stop 2:00 / 4:00	Actual Start / Stop
The Company's Creative Past	15	2:00 / 2:15	_____ / _____
Break for Creative Expression	15	2:15 / 2:30	_____ / _____
Creativity Climate Survey	20	2:30 / 2:50	_____ / _____
Road to Success	30	2:50 / 3:20	_____ / _____
The Company's Creative Future	20	3:20 / 3:40	_____ / _____
Break	10	3:40 / 3:50	_____ / _____
Thumbprints	10	3:50 / 4:00	_____ / _____

4. Flash Your Creativity	Minutes 1 hr.	Start / Stop 4:00 / 5:00	Actual Start / Stop
Brainstorming	5	4:00 / 4:05	_____ / _____
What Can You Do?	20	4:05 / 4:25	_____ / _____
Lighting Others' Creativity	10	4:25 / 4:35	_____ / _____
Conclusion	25	4:35 / 5:00	_____ / _____

Materials and Equipment Checklist

☐ Your facilitator notes.

☐ Participant materials.

☐ Name tents (p. 46).

☐ *Flash Your Creativity* flashlights (penlight flashlights—one per participant).

☐ Flipchart and pens to be used at your discretion.

☐ Overhead projector, screen and pens.

☐ Overhead transparencies.

☐ Audio cassette player, creativity-sparking musical tapes.

☐ Box of crayons for every 3 or 4 participants.

☐ Small can of Play-Doh for every 3 or 4 participants.

☐ A crisp one dollar bill and a quarter.

☐ Materials needed to stimulate senses as defined by you.

☐ Toys of your choice from your toy box.

☐ Idea Sparker Cards (p. 291).

☐ Samples of kid's fun food (e.g., Pop Rocks, Cracker Jacks, Bazooka bubble gum).

☐ Group table tents (pp. 284-288).

☐ Turtle Awards (p. 289).

☐ Ink pads (and disposable towelettes to clean fingers).

☐ *Road to Success Script* (pp. 225-232) and slides (p. 292).

☐ Masking tape.

☐ Blank envelopes, one per participant.

☐ Materials for optional activities of your choice:

_____

_____

_____

Suggestions for Your "Toy Table"

☐ Coloring books.

☐ Play-Doh.

☐ Jump rope.

☐ Soft Frisbee.

☐ Kaleidoscopes.

☐ Yo-yo.

☐ Pickup sticks.

☐ Jacks.

☐ Nerf ball.

☐ Clay.

☐ Koosh ball.

☐ Puzzles.

☐ Paddle ball.

☐ Marbles.

☐ Juggling items.

☐ Prisms.

☐ Harmonica.

☐ Bubbles.

☐ Colored chalk.

☐ Kazoo.

☐ Crayons.
   (Especially the neon, glitter, metallic swirl, scented, fluorescent or any others that are new on the market).

Participant Materials

The masters for all participant materials can be found in Chapter 6. You will need to make one handout for each participant. In addition, as mentioned in Chapter 2, you need to decide how to bind these materials. Since this session has numerous handouts, you may consider a small three-ring binder or have them spiral bound. Another approach, less expensive and totally within your control is to use pocket folders. Divide the materials into their four modules and put a cover page on each (perhaps color coded). Then place all four smaller packets in a pocket folder.

- ☐ Cover Page (p. 135).
- ☐ Questioning Creativity? (pp. 136-137).
- ☐ Meet the Creative Me (p. 138).
- ☐ Can Creativity Be Defined? (p. 139).
- ☐ Do You Know. . . ? (p. 140).
- ☐ Right-Brain/Left-Brain? (p. 141).
- ☐ Nine Uncreative Boxes (p. 142).
- ☐ Unbox Your Creativity—A (p. 143).
- ☐ Unbox Your Creativity—B (p. 144).
- ☐ Unbox Your Creativity—C (p. 145).
- ☐ Unbox Your Creativity—D (p. 146).
- ☐ Unbox Your Creativity—E (p. 147).
- ☐ Idea Sparker (p. 148).
- ☐ My Creative Climate (p. 149).
- ☐ A Spectrum of Creativity Techniques (p. 150).
- ☐ Risky Business (p. 151).
- ☐ Your Creative Spectrum— Compare and Combine (p. 152).
- ☐ Your Creative Spectrum— Risk Taking (p. 153).
- ☐ Your Creative Spectrum— Expand and Shrink (p. 154).
- ☐ Your Creative Spectrum— Ask What's Good? and What If? (p. 155).

- ☐ Your Creative Spectrum— Transform Your Viewpoint (p. 156).
- ☐ Your Creative Spectrum— In Another Sequence (p. 157).
- ☐ Your Creative Spectrum— Visit Other Places (p. 158).
- ☐ Your Creative Spectrum— Incubate (pp. 159-160).
- ☐ Your Creative Spectrum— Trigger Concepts (p. 161).
- ☐ Your Creative Spectrum— Youth's Advantage (p. 162).
- ☐ The Company's Creative Past (p. 163).
- ☐ Creativity Climate Survey (pp. 164-166).
- ☐ Opened Climates (pp. 167-168).
- ☐ Killer Phrases (p. 169).
- ☐ Where Can Creativity Flourish? (p. 170).
- ☐ Brainstorming (pp.171-172).
- ☐ What Can You Do? (p. 173).
- ☐ Lighting Others' Creativity (pp.174-175).
- ☐ Creatively Yours (p. 176).
- ☐ Reading List (p. 177).
- ☐ Session Evaluation (p. 178).

Overhead Transparencies

You will use the first 17 overhead transparencies for this workshop. Make one of each. We recommend that you "make them colorful" in some way. You may simply color them with a permanent marker or add self-adhering colored film. They could also be scanned into your computer and computer colored. For a professional appearance, be sure to put them into transparency frames.

- ☐ Define Creativity (p. 265).

- ☐ Making of the New (p. 266).

- ☐ Right-Brain/Left-Brain? (p. 267).

- ☐ Whole-Brain Thinking (p. 268).

- ☐ Discovery Consists (p. 269).

- ☐ Nine Uncreative Boxes (p. 270).

- ☐ Opportunityisnowhere (p. 271).

- ☐ Unbox Your Creativity (p. 272).

- ☐ A Spectrum of Creativity Techniques (p. 273).

- ☐ Turtle Race (p. 274).

- ☐ The Company's Creative Past (p. 275).

- ☐ Where Can Creativity Flourish? (p. 276).

- ☐ Brainstorming (p. 277).

- ☐ Candle With Quote (p. 278).

- ☐ Creative Flashes (p. 279).

- ☐ Come Out of Your Shell (p. 280).

- ☐ Flower (p. 281).

Flipchart

There is one flipchart to prepare for this workshop, and it should look like this:

Objectives

- Define creativity.
- Identify the boxes that prevent creativity.
- Design your creative environment.
- Use a variety of creativity techniques.
- Relate risk taking and creativity.
- Relate creativity to company culture.
- Encourage others' creativity.
- Use creativity skills on the job.

A reminder

Creativity can be a threatening topic for some. Prepare yourself to teach this topic differently from any other. Because you'll be conducting unique activities that tap into a participant's right brain, it may take time for them to feel comfortable with your techniques. Therefore, you may observe discomfort, may need to wait longer for responses, may need to be prepared with starter responses, may need to justify an activity or may need to offer more reinforcement than usual.

Be persistent and patient and remain enthusiastic. They'll soon get into right-brain thinking and realize that they can learn while having fun. The better you prepare, the more successful you will be.

Training Plan

1. In the Dark

Purpose   The purpose of this module is to introduce some interesting facts about creativity and to push participants to right-brain thinking.

Materials needed
- Penlight.
- Name tents (p. 46).
- Crayons and paper.
- Dollar bill, quarter.
- Group table tents (pp. 284-288).

- *Nine Uncreative Boxes* (p. 142).
- *Unbox Your Creativity* (pp. 143-147).

Handouts

- *Questioning Creativity* (pp. 136-137).
- *Meet the Creative Me* (p. 138).
- *Can Creativity Be Defined?* (p. 139).
- *Do You Know. . . ?* (p. 140).
- *Right-Brain/Left-Brain?* (p. 141).

Overheads

- *Define Creativity* (p. 265).
- *Right-Brain/Left-Brain?* (p. 267).
- *Whole-Brain Thinking* (p. 268).
- *Making of the New* (p. 266).
- *Discovery Consists* (p. 269).
- *Nine Uncreative Boxes* (p. 270).
- *Opportunityisnowhere* (p. 271).
- *Unbox Your Creativity* (p. 272).

Workshop Agenda

1. In the Dark	Minutes 3 hrs.	Start / Stop 8:00 / 11:00	Actual Start / Stop
Introduction	20	8:00 / 8:20	_____ / _____
Meet the Creative Me	20	8:20 / 8:40	_____ / _____
Objectives	5	8:40 / 8:45	_____ / _____
Can Creativity Be Defined?	20	8:45 / 9:05	_____ / _____
Do You Know. . . ?	20	9:05 / 9:25	_____ / _____
Right-Brain/Left-Brain?	10	9:25 / 9:35	_____ / _____
Toy Break	15	9:35 / 9:50	_____ / _____
Nine Uncreative Boxes	15	9:50 / 10:05	_____ / _____
Unbox Your Creativity	45	10:05 / 10:50	_____ / _____
Out of Your Box Break	10	10:50 / 11:00	_____ / _____

1. In the Dark (8:00 to 11:00)

FACILITATOR COMMENTARY

00:20   **Introduction**

Begin when all participants are seated and it's time to start the session. Softly start the mood music and turn on your flashlight. Then, turn off the room lights and begin the session in the dark.

 WELCOME participants to *Widen Your Spectrum.*

 SAY: You're about to enter a world of color and laughter; ideas and fun—your own private world of creativity, an experiment of YOU.

- Within each of us exists an infinite capacity for creating ideas and nurturing them to the point of innovation. Today you will explore how we, as individuals, have boxed ourselves in, prevented the flow of ideas, inhibited creativity and kept ourselves in the dark.

- You may choose to remain in the dark, or to ignite your creative spark. Today I challenge you to harness your creative energy as we explore numerous theory-based creativity techniques. You'll learn to focus your creativity. There is a ray of hope.

- Some of you have already begun to flash your creativity (if some participants have found and are using the flashlight). Take a few moments now to explore it more. You have a flashlight in front of you. Use it to be creative.

 WAIT for participants to use the flashlights.

Give the participants a moment to "be creative" with their flashlights. Some will not feel comfortable and ask questions. Just assure them they should be creative with their flashlights. Wait about 30 seconds to one minute, then continue talking.

DO NOT TURN ON THE LIGHTS YET!

 SAY:

Creativity doesn't just happen. It is not available on demand even though we are all born with creative potential.

The success of creativity is a learned process. You can transform your black and white thinking into colorful innovations.

Therefore, I challenge you to begin to widen and brighten your spectrum. Welcome to the colorful world of creativity!

Turn the *LIGHTS ON* and the *MUSIC OFF.*

ASK how many of the participants were uncomfortable while trying to be creative with the flashlights?

 Expect that many are going to admit that they were uncomfortable. You might encounter strong resistance and negative comments to this activity (e.g., "It was too contrived." "It was hokey." "I don't see what it had to do with creativity.") Listen to such questions earnestly accepting the discomfort felt by the people giving the feedback. Do not avoid these issues—this is imperative to the success of the entire session. You must address them. The following will help you.

SAY:

The exercise was designed to be somewhat uncomfortable. The concepts of creativity are new to most people, and it's difficult to perform them "on demand."

Throughout the session you will encounter experiences that will take you farther and farther into your creative mode, or right brain. The session is loaded with creativity techniques. Traditional work and education stress the left-brain skills (e.g., logic, math, organization, etc.) My job as facilitator is to push you as far right as you can go. New skills must be practiced.

The first handout, *Questioning Creativity?* (pp. 136–137), may address some of your issues. You may take a look at that later.

ASK: Why were they uncomfortable?

LISTEN for answers such as:

- It makes some feel different or foolish.

- Some will be lost because the instructions were so open-ended. People are used to getting detailed instructions.

- It was threatening, risky and scary to some. People fear the unknown—they fear failure.

SAY: All of these responses are the boxes we've put ourselves in which inhibit creativity.

Reinforce anyone who enjoyed the activity, yet be empathetic and understanding with those who didn't.

INTRODUCE yourself to the group.

SAY: We will take the next few minutes to meet one another.

00:20   **Meet the Creative Me**

 TELL each participant to complete the *Meet the Creative Me* (p. 138) handout. Model your answers to these questions to ease any discomfort they may have in opening up their creative side to the group. Use the sample answers provided in the Trainer's Notes (p. 195) or better yet, create your own!

GROUP ACTIVITY

 TELL participants to take four to five minutes to complete the page. Then have them use their answers to introduce themselves to the large group. We recommend that you start with random volunteers instead of the typical going around the table for two reasons:

- It's unique, creative, different from the typical—which allows you to model what this session is all about.

- If some people are feeling uncomfortable, they can volunteer when they feel more comfortable. Therefore, you are modeling adult learning theory practices—allowing people to feel in control of their environment.

ASK if anyone felt uncomfortable using this format for introductions. You may wish to discuss the following points:

- This was a right-brain way of introducing self.

- Some people feel uncomfortable using the right brain to reveal "self." They feel naked, unprotected.

ASK if anyone fell into the trap of working from the left brain or logical side. Don't expect an answer to this particular question, but follow quickly asking for a show of hands:

How many of you felt:

     – a need to go from top to bottom?

     – a need to stick to a theme?

     – there was a right or wrong answer?

     – your creativity would be judged?

     – all the blanks had to be filled in?

     – you had to finish?

ASK why they think this may have occurred.

REFER to the bottom of the handout and ***ASK*** for their thoughts about how the quotation by William James (1842–1910, psychologist and philosopher) relates to what just occurred. Use the discussion to illustrate these points:

- People can change.

- Our attitudes affect the way we behave.

- If we think we are something, then we will be just that.

 ASK what's the worst thing that can happen to you during this session? Expect answers such as:

- I will be asked to do something I cannot do.

- I will look stupid or foolish.

- I will be asked to do something I do not believe in.

- I will not be creative.

SAY in summary:

Creative people will be creative, no matter which job they perform. There is a company which has the following rule: "The only rule in this company is that there are no rules." In this session, there are no rules. Walk around when you like. Observe and try activities in the room at your leisure. Take breaks when you need them. Sit on the floor if you like. We are going to push your creativity to the limits at first. By the end of the session, you will be able to harness your creativity and use it more than you have in the past.

INDIVIDUAL ACTIVITY

 REFER to the name tents activity portion of the *Meet the Creative Me* handout (p. 138) and have anyone who has not yet completed it do so now, making the following points:

- Print the names they wish to be called (yes, it could even be their new names from this exercise).

- They may decorate it with the crayons or markers or anything else they see around the room. Yours may be a model decorated with flowers, shapes, rainbows or whatever moves you.

- An optional, but fun continuation of this project, is to say that in addition, they can put the name of their inner child on the inside of the table tent! Do this only if the group is ready for it!

Move on. Do not wait for participants to decorate their name tents. (A sample name tent appears on p. 46.)

00:05   **Objectives**

REFER to the flipchart where you have listed the objectives of the session. They may be similar to the following. However, if you have customized the session in any way, be sure that they are all applicable. As a result of this full day session participants will be able to:

- Define creativity.

- Identify the boxes that prevent your creativity.

- Design your individualized creative environment.

- Use a variety of creativity techniques to encourage creative efforts.

- Understand the relationship between taking risks and creativity.

- Relate creativity to the company's culture and future needs.

- Encourage and support others' creative efforts.

- Use creativity skills learned in the session on the job.

POST the flipchart on the wall during the next break.

GROUP ACTIVITY

00:20   **Can Creativity Be Defined?**

TELL participants to break into groups according to height. Do not give any other instructions. Allow plenty of time for them to figure out what this means. Some may get hung up on "doing it right." Remind them, "No rules." We impose our own rules. There are many ways to break into groups "according to height." (e.g., line up and split into X groups; tall, average and short into three groups; one tall, one average and one short in each group; or anyway because we all "have height.")

SAY as a summary:

- This is another example of boxing ourselves in as we search for the rules.

- There are many "right ways to do things."

- The point is there is no "one correct way."

SAY to introduce the activity:

Let's define creativity. We need to know it when we see it. In your groups, come up with a definition and a description or a symbol for creativity. Be prepared to share your ideas with the larger group and feel free to use the flipchart if you wish.

You may use the *Can Creativity Be Defined?* (p. 139) handout to record your ideas.

 ASK representatives from the groups to share their ideas.

 USE the overhead, *Define Creativity* (p. 265), to record their responses.

Share the definition on the overhead, *Making of the New* (p. 266), and say, this is Mike Vance's (The Disney Corporation) definition.

Other definitions to guide the discussion are:

- The ability to bring about a new idea or invention.

- The ability to be original.

- The ability to bring something into being; give rise to.

 REFER to the quotation at the bottom of the handout, "Everything that can be invented has been invented," by Charles H. Duell (Director of U.S. Patent Office, 1899).

FACILITATOR COMMENTARY

 SAY:

Duell's quotation is humorous, but he meant it most seriously. Compare what he is saying to, "There is nothing new under the sun," a quotation from the Bible, Ecclesiastes 1:9.

Point out that both quotations illustrate an important fact about creativity—it takes what is and makes it different to bring about a new idea or invention.

 If you have time you may wish to incorporate discussion around either of the following points:

- Point out that during the past few years, over one-half of the U.S. patents went to non-American people. Ask for comments on this fact. Are we getting less creative? Or has everything been invented?

- If you conducted a *Creativity Needs Assessment* (p. 254) prior to the session, you may wish to incorporate any appropriate information at this time.

FACILITATOR COMMENTARY

00:20   **Do You Know. . . ?**

 Refer to the *Do You Know. . . ?* handout (p. 140).

 SAY:

We have been exploring the nature of creativity, and this page provides a format for you to complete as I review some interesting facts about creativity. Please use the lines to take notes.

- Using the Trainer's Notes for *Do You Know. . . ?* (p. 201-202), read each item in order (from top to bottom, starting with number 11) asking, "Do you know. . ."

 ASK if they would like to discuss any of the points further.

 TELL participants to turn the page. If no one has asked about the numbering of questions—ask them why? The point to make is that we're often afraid to ask questions. We don't want to seem "stupid." Remember, there are no rules.

00:10   **Right-Brain/Left-Brain?**

REFER to the *Right-Brain/Left-Brain?* handout (p. 141) and *USE* the overhead, *Right-Brain/Left-Brain?* (p. 267), to discuss Split-Brain Theory.

SAY:

There has been much talk about "Right-Brain and Left-Brain Theory." It is true that the cortex of the cerebrum's left hemisphere assumes responsibility for analytical functions, and the cortex for the cerebrum's right hemisphere assumes responsibility for the imaginative functions. But it isn't that black and white. The two hemispheres are more similar than different, and almost every mental process requires that they work together.

Therefore, keep in mind that these are just labels, terms, and that there are no separate compartments in our brains that store or process information that simplistically.

Instead, we need to understand that there are two ways of thinking that can be called right-brain and left-brain thinking.

We cannot do both types of thinking at the same time, and we shift from one side to the other constantly.

The most successful people are those who can easily shift from one thinking style to the other.

REFER to the overhead, pointing to the words, and *SAY:*

All too often, people in business find themselves stuck in the left side of the brain. On the left side, we have the words: Analytical, Verbal, Sequential, Objective, Cause and Effect, Science and Math, and Logical. These terms sound, and are, very business like.

On the right side of this person's brain, we find the words: Intuitive, Visual, Timeless, Subjective, Spontaneous, Arts and Music, and Emotional.

ASK:

- Using these words and phrases as a guide, how do you describe people who are mostly right-brain thinkers? (Expect to hear words like: flaky, weird, artsy, off the wall, etc.)

- How would you describe people who are mostly left-brain thinkers? (They may use words like: nerds, bookworms, techies, etc.)

SAY:

The point is that you want to achieve balance. The myth that the left brain is a computer and the right brain is a crystal ball can be positive. It encourages all of us to experiment with different ways of thinking.

Remember, those who are most successful use both sides of their brains. This is referred to as "whole-brain thinking."

Try this exercise with me. Please stand and tighten your right arm. Tighten it more. Tighter now. Does it hurt? Keep tightening it. (Someone will finally say that it hurts.)

ASK:

Now, what if that arm were in a cast? Could you tighten it? Could you exercise it?

SAY:

No. If you tighten your arm constantly, it gets tired. If you can't exercise it, it gets weak. We need a sequence of the two—tightening and loosening, working and resting our arm muscles.

Likewise, we need to work and rest both sides of our brain. We use isometrics to exercise our muscles. Just as the golfer practices the swing and putting skills, we need to exercise our brains, too. We need to be able to move more freely from the right to the left and back again.

Since we have had less formal training in using the right brain, you will be getting plenty of right-brain exercise during this session.

REFER to the cartoon on the overhead, *Whole-Brain Thinking* (p. 268), and close this session with a laugh.

 You may add this point if you have time:

Split-brain research has shown us much, particularly that the left side of the brain controls the right side of the body and vice versa. Studies have shown that listening to a phone conversation with the left ear allows the listener to better listen for tone and emotional responses. Conversely, listening with the right ear gives the listener a more objective message. Experts who study body language contend that when people shift their eyes left during a conversation, they are searching for feeling responses. When they shift their eyes right, they're more likely to be looking for analytical responses.

00:15

Toy Break

 Adult learning theory requires that participants are comfortable. You should encourage your participants to take informal breaks for any reason, at any time. However, you must still take formal breaks at least every 90 minutes. That time is now. Give participants a 15 minute break.

This break should be announced as a "toy break." Draw attention to the "Toy Table," a table on one side of the room where you have placed a variety of toys for the participants to play with.

The objectives are to:

*   Help participants get in touch with their childhood, when they more than likely felt more free to be creative.

*   Release the child that likes to play. Play leads to creativity.

*   Encourage participants to get out of the boxes that prevent them from being creative.

*   Relaxation and play times are conducive to right-brain thinking, allowing ideas to surface more easily.

For ideas, refer to *Suggestions for Your Toy Table* in Chapter 2.

 REFER to the *Discovery Consists* overhead with the quote by Szent-Györgyi (p. 269) to bring people back from the break.

00:15   **Nine Uncreative Boxes**

FACILITATOR COMMENTARY

 Refer to the Trainer's Notes for *Getting Out of the Box* (p. 205) for detailed instructions for this exercise.

 ASK: Why aren't we more creative?

- We have routines that guide us and provide structure to operate on a daily basis. If we got up in the morning and tried to brainstorm 50 ways to cook an egg—we'd never get to work. We need routines.

- We have developed attitudes or "boxes" that trap our creativity. We create many of these for ourselves. We box ourselves in with these attitudes.

 DEMONSTRATE the following example, as described in the Trainer's Notes.

Display a dollar bill and a quarter and ask one participant to balance the quarter on the edge of the dollar bill. Praise creative solutions to this problem. After several attempts, provide the solution.

Fold the dollar accordion style and lay the quarter on top. This is a simple example of how we are boxed in by the question and our paradigms.

 REFER to the *Nine Uncreative Boxes* handout (p. 142) and the overhead, *Nine Uncreative Boxes* (p. 270). Use a pointer to focus participants' attention on each box as you speak about it.

 SAY:

Just as we began our work together in the dark, there are nine boxes that we can allow ourselves to be locked within. The *Nine Uncreative Boxes* handout lists and illustrates these. Let's review them one by one. Color any of these that you feel box in your creativity.

- Use the definitions from the Trainer's Notes for *Getting Out of the Box* (p. 206-207).

00:45   **Unbox Your Creativity**

GROUP ACTIVITY

?   *ASK:*

Have you identified your boxes—those attitudes that keep you in the dark and prevent you from being as creative as you can be?

 SAY that you would like them to spend the next 25 minutes (or less if you are short of time) working in pairs or trios with others who have identified the same uncreative boxes as you.

The five page handout entitled *Unbox Your Creativity* (pp. 143–147) matches the nine uncreative boxes. They should find someone and do the activity stated for one or two of the boxes.

 SAY:

During this activity you will explore how to get out of your boxes—how to unbox your creativity and bring it into the light.

There is time flexibility within this activity. If you are short of time, participants can address only one box. If you have ample time they can complete up to three activities.

Be sure to save 20 minutes at the end to debrief the activity so that small groups can share some of their ideas.

You may use the following information for each of the activities in any way you wish to guide the discussion.

Option   To provide ideas and insight to the exercises, you may include the information from the Trainer's Notes (pp. 208-212) for this exercise. However, participants may have more and better information to share as a result of the activity.

- Tear Apart Time Trapped Boxes!
- Rip the Risky Business Zone!
- Perforate the Perfectionist's Problem!
- End Wright or Wrong Thinking!
- Empty the Self-Fulfilling Prophecy!
- Bust Bottom-Line Thinking!
- Pull Apart Environmental Pollution!
- Eliminate Only One Right Answer!
- Ripple Calm Waters!

00:10   **Out of Your Box Break**

 ANNOUNCE that they will have a 10 minute Out of Your Box Break.

- This can mean anything they wish it to mean!

 DISPLAY the overhead, *Opportunityisnowhere* (p. 271), to bring participants back from break.

 ASK:

What does this say?

- Wait for their responses.

- Make these points:

  - Opportunity is "now here," though some of us may read it as "no where."

  - You just have to see it that way. It's a matter of perception.

  - Isn't it interesting that the exact same letters can mean the opposite, depending upon how we read it? Our view of creativity, work and life can be viewed in the same way!

 SAY:

If you want to see something that will really boggle your mind, this diagram can be seen in four different formations.

 DISPLAY the overhead, *Unbox Your Creativity* (p. 272), and have participants list what they see: a cube with a smaller cube cut out; a cube with a small cube attached; a room with a box in the corner; a room with a cave-like cube room beyond. You may need to turn the transparency upside down so that the four formations can be seen by most people.

2. See the Light

Purpose	In this module, participants will be introduced to ten creativity techniques and will explore the idea of risk taking.
Materials needed	• Idea Sparker Cards (p. 291).
	• Handout *Idea Sparker* (p. 148).
	• Handout *My Creative Climate* (p. 149).
	• Handout *A Spectrum of Creativity Techniques* (p. 150).
	• Handout *Your Creative Spectrum* (pp. 152-162).
	• Handout *Risky Business* (p. 151).
	• Overhead *A Spectrum of Creativity Techniques* (p. 273).
	• Overhead *Turtle Race* (p. 274).
	• *Turtle Awards* (p. 289).
	• Group table tents (pp. 284-288).

Workshop Agenda

2. See the Light	Minutes 3 hrs.	Start / Stop 11:00 / 2:00	Actual Start / Stop
Idea Sparker	10	11:00 / 11:10	_____ / _____
My Creative Climate	15	11:10 / 11:25	_____ / _____
A Spectrum of Creativity Techniques	35	11:25 / 12:00	_____ / _____
Lunch: Take a Risk to Lunch	60	12:00 / 1:00	_____ / _____
Share Risky Business	10	1:00 / 1:10	_____ / _____
Your Creative Spectrum Practice	50	1:10 / 2:00	_____ / _____

2. See the Light (11:00 to 2:00)

FACILITATOR COMMENTARY

00:10   **Idea Sparker**

 SAY:

It is important to exercise your mind. You can strengthen your creativity skills, by reading creative books, visiting unusual places (like a toy store when you really have no toys to purchase), reading magazines outside your profession, using Idea Sparker Cards or other creativity enhancing activities. If you practice making the shift from left-brain to right-brain thinking daily, you will strengthen your ability to be creative when you need to come up with new ideas.

INDIVIDUAL ACTIVITY

  REFER to the *Idea Sparker* handout (p. 148). Have them complete *Color-Blind* (card no. 7, from the *Idea Sparker Cards,* if available) working two minutes alone.

GROUP ACTIVITY

 HAVE them work two minutes with a partner and ask volunteers to share some of their responses.

 ASK:

• What happened when you worked with partners?

• What does this say about creativity?

 LISTEN for responses such as:

• Two heads are better than one.

• Concept of "building on" others' ideas to create new ones.

• Many of us need stimuli to enhance our own creativity.

FACILITATOR COMMENTARY

00:15   **My Creative Climate**

     SAY:

In part one of the session, we explored ways to break out of our uncreative boxes. Now, let's turn our attention to building the type of environment that encourages and rewards creative efforts.

Most creative people understand the need for a specific environment or routine that enhances their creative abilities. Some famous people have shared what "keeps their creative juice flowing."

For example, Mozart (18th-century Austrian composer) needed to exercise before he composed music. Dr. Samuel Johnson (18th-century English author) wanted a purring cat, orange peels and tea in his creative environment. Immanuel Kant (German philosopher) liked to work in bed at times with blankets arranged in a special way. Hart Crane (20th-century American poet) played jazz loudly on a Victrola and Johann Schiller (18th-century German poet) needed to fill his desk with rotten apples. Archimedes (ancient Greek mathematician and inventor) recognized the importance of relaxing and often solved his most difficult problems in a hot bath.   And finally, Samuel Cray of super-computer fame, digs a tunnel beneath his house when he feels blocked from creative ideas.

Get in touch with what makes you feel creative. Is it certain scents (the change of seasons, cinnamon, baking bread), sights (sunrise, mountains, vacation pictures, flowers), sounds (ocean waves, jazz music, silence), tastes (chocolate, oranges, cappuccino) or feels (cool glass, comfortable sweatshirt, spring breeze)? What makes you feel more creative?

     REFER to the *My Creative Climate* (p. 149) handout. Share your own creative climate needs as an example. Jot them down here before the session.

     TELL participants to:

- Take five minutes to complete their *My Creative Climate* handout, (p. 149).

- Share ideas as a large group.

FACILITATOR COMMENTARY

00:35

A Spectrum of Creativity Techniques

REFER to the Trainer's Script (pp. 219-222), overhead (p. 273), and handout (p. 150) for *A Spectrum of Creativity Techniques*. To help participants stay focused, use the revealing technique (place a piece of paper under the transparency and gradually pull the paper down the transparency) to uncover each technique.

SAY that as you briefly explain each of the following ten techniques, you would like them to write a few notes.

- Compare and Combine.
- Risk Taking.
- Expand and Shrink.
- Ask, What's Good? and What If?
- Transform Your Viewpoint.
- In Another Sequence.
- Visit Other Places.
- Incubate.
- Trigger Concepts.
- Youth's Advantage.

1:00

Take a Risk to Lunch

SAY that it is time for lunch and that you would like everyone to take a risk during the lunch break.

- You may define "risk" in any way that you choose.
- If you think you will do something unbelievable, take the *Risky Business* (p. 151) handout and have a witness sign it.
- You should be prepared to report back about your risk.
- Remember to return within the hour.

During lunch you will need to:

- Prepare the *Turtle Awards* (p. 289).
- Place the group table tents (*Is a closet poet, Would like to write a book, Enjoys daydreaming, Likes to play with clay, Has painted a picture*) around the room where five small groups may gather (pp. 284-288).
- Set up the *Road to Success* slides (if available; p. 292).
- Place child-like unusual snacks on the tables (e.g., Cracker Jacks, Bazooka bubble gum, Pop Rocks).

00:10   **Risky Business**

 ASK:

- How many of you took a risk at lunch today? Facilitate the discussion, allowing everyone who wishes to share what they did with the group.

- How do the risks differ?

- Are some risks less risky? Some more calculated? Some crazier?

 REFER to the overhead, *Turtle Race* (p. 274). Let them know that you have Turtle Awards for the risk takers. To end the discussion, announce that those who wish to continue the discussion about risk taking may do so during the next activity.

 You may wish to fill in the risk-takers' names on the Turtle Awards during the next activity.

GROUP ACTIVITY

00:50   **Your Creative Spectrum Practice**

 REFER to the *Your Creative Spectrum* handouts (pp. 152-162).

 SAY that you would like them to work in small groups. Once they reach their small groups they should decide which of the ten techniques they would like to practice. If time permits, they may complete two activities. Once in their small groups they will have a total of 25 minutes. They should select a technique and complete the activity as addressed on the specific technique handout.

- There are five table tents (*Is a closet poet, Would like to write a book, Enjoys daydreaming, Likes to play with clay, Has painted a picture*) around the room. Select the area that most represents you and go to that spot.

- Once there are ____ people in a group, move to your second choice. (Establish a maximum number in each group. For example, if you have 18 people, you might say, "no more than 4 people in a group; after 4 people are in a group, move to your second choice.")

MONITOR the groups:

- Move from group to group making sure they each know what they are to do.

- Circulate a couple of times to answer questions or keep them on track.

GIVE two time signals. Announce that their time is half over after about 13 minutes. Also, announce when five minutes of their time is left so they can begin to wrap up.

SAY:

Let's get back together as a large group to discover what each group did and what you learned. Ask each group to report their experience.

Watch the time closely to ensure that each team has time to report their experience.

Notes

- _____
- _____
- _____
- _____
- _____
- _____
- _____
- _____
- _____
- _____
- _____
- _____
- _____
- _____
- _____
- _____

3. Light Your Company's Creativity

Purpose   In this module, participants will have the opportunity to measure the creativity climate in which they work. After exploring why individuals as well as companies may become unable to use their creative potential, they will consider ways to improve their creativity climate in the future.

Materials needed

- Handout *The Company's Creative Past* (p. 163).

- Handout *Creativity Climate Survey* (pp. 164-166).

- Handout *Opened Climates* (p. 167-168).

- Handout *Killer Phrases* (p. 169).

- Handout *Where Can Creativity Flourish?* (p. 170).

- Overhead *The Company's Creative Past* (p. 275).

- Overhead *Where Can Creativity Flourish?* (p. 276).

- Overhead *Flower* (p. 281).

- *Road to Success Script* (pp. 225-232).

- *Road to Success* slides (if available; p. 292) and projector.

- Organizational items that depict its creative past (e.g., photos, awards, newspaper clippings).

- Jump rope.

- Frisbee.

- Clay.

- Ink pads.

Workshop Agenda

3. Light Your Company's Creativity	Minutes 2 hrs.	Start / Stop 2:00 / 4:00	Actual Start / Stop
The Company's Creative Past	15	2:00 / 2:15	_____ / _____
Break for Creative Expression	15	2:15 / 2:30	_____ / _____
Creativity Climate Survey	20	2:30 / 2:50	_____ / _____
Road to Success	30	2:50 / 3:20	_____ / _____
The Company's Creative Future	20	3:20 / 3:40	_____ / _____
Break	10	3:40 / 3:50	_____ / _____
Thumbprints	10	3:50 / 4:00	_____ / _____

3. Light Your Company's Creativity (2:00 to 4:00)

00:15   **The Company's Creative Past**

FACILITATOR COMMENTARY

 SAY:

Our company has been creative in the past, and it's that creativity that brought us this far.

I've brought some reminders that may jog your memory (hold them up one at a time as you identify them, which might include old pictures, newspaper clippings, old ads, trophies, products, expansion information, etc.).

 PAIR up with the person next to you and list as many of our company's past creative actions as you can in five minutes on *The Company's Creative Past* (p. 163) handout.

Now let's go around and get one example from each pair.

 REFER to the overhead, *The Company's Creative Past* (p. 275), and write each example as it is given.

 ASK:

• What does this list tell us?

• How can we summarize where we've been as a creative company?

00:15   **Break for Creative Expression**

 Have some of the more activity-oriented toys (jump rope, Frisbee, clay, Koosh ball, bubbles) available and encourage participants to re-energize themselves by "playing."

00:20   **Creativity Climate Survey**

 To save time you may choose to send the survey to participants to complete as pre-work.

 REFER participants to the *Creativity Climate Survey* handout (pp. 164-166). Have individuals complete the survey and score it.

 ASK:

- What are the highest scores?
- What are the lowest scores?
- What does this tell us about our present day creativity climate?

 REFER to the *Opened Climates* handout (pp. 167-168), and suggest that this list provides ideas of what we can all do to open the creativity climate. It can be used as a resource for them during *The Company's Creative Future* activity on page 81.

 SAY:

Our next activity may give you some insight about how a company's creativity climate can close.

00:30   **Road to Success**

FACILITATOR COMMENTARY

 SAY:

I'm going to read a short story to you. During that time please feel free to color, shape clay, doodle or just sit back and imagine this happening in this city, in this company, in your department, to you.

 Read the *Road to Success Script* and show the slides (p. 292), if available. If the slides are not available, end with the *Flower* overhead (p. 281).

 SAY:

Today you've experienced two kinds of creative darkness:

- The world of uncertainty where we trap ourselves and keep creativity stifled.
- The blows that come from the outside world that beat down our creativity and can even destroy it.

 ASK:

- How did you feel at the end of the script? (Expect to hear depressed, upset, angry.)

SAY:

It can be difficult to foster our own, let alone others', creativity. Yet, it is so easy to squash and even punish creativity in those we touch.

An awareness of what creativity is and how it can be nurtured will help us avoid pushing everyone down the tried and true road to success as depicted in the story.

Let's examine how we can do just that in the next activity.

00:20   **The Company's Creative Future**

SAY:

Let's spend a few minutes examining what we as individuals can do to encourage a more creative climate. One of the things we can do is be careful of what we say.

INDIVIDUAL ACTIVITY

REFER to the *Killer Phrases* handout (p. 169) and have participants list as many as they can. Give them some to get started:

"It won't work!" "We tried that last year!" "That's not the way we do things!" "We're not quite ready for that!" "It's not practical!" "Top management will never go for it!" "Ideas are a dime a dozen!"

SAY:

Let's read some of your phrases. (Encourage everyone to read them faster and louder at the same time.)

That's quite a list!

I think the least we can do is get rid of all creativity killer phrases. (Set the wastebasket in the middle of the room.)

Rip that page out of your materials, wad it up and toss those killer phrases away for good.

Now let's come up with some positive steps we can take as an organization. Turn once again to the *Opened Climates* handout (pp. 167-168).

Organize yourselves into six groups. Try to find someone with whom you have not worked today. Assign one of the categories— Open-minded, Perceptive, Equal, Nurturing, Encouraging and Descriptive—to each of the teams. Have them expand on these ideas or list others of their own.

REFER them to the *Where Can Creativity Flourish?* handout (p. 170) to record their ideas.

ASK:

- What ideas did you think of?

- How many of these can we do as a company?

As participants are discussing their ideas, you may list them on the overhead, *Where Can Creativity Flourish?* (p. 276), if you wish.

ASK: So if we do these things, how does our company's creative future look?

Lead a cheer and take a break!

(Play music during the break and the next activity.)

00:10   **Break**

GROUP ACTIVITY

00:10   **Thumbprints**

When participants return from break, have ink pads at each table. Have participants press their thumbs on the pads and put their thumbprints any place on their materials. Ask them to make their thumbprints into something (e.g., a bug, a car, a flying saucer. . .) and let them play for a few minutes.

Have them share their creations with the large group.

You may skip this activity if you are short of time. You could also make it a part of the break.

4. Flash Your Creativity

Purpose

In this module, participants will learn brainstorming techniques and identify steps they can take to become more creative. In addition, they will see how to encourage creativity in others.

Materials needed

- Handout *Brainstorming* (pp. 171-172).

- Handout *What Can You Do?* (p. 173).

- Handout *Lighting Others Creativity* (pp. 174-175).

- Handout *Creatively Yours* (p. 176).

- Handout *Reading List* (p. 177).

- Handout *Session Evaluation* (p. 178).

- Overhead *Brainstorming* (p. 277).

- Overhead *Candle With Quote* (p. 278).

- Overhead *Creative Flashes* (p. 279).

- Overhead *Come Out of Your Shell* (p. 280).

- Overhead *Flower* (p. 281).

- Envelopes—one per participant.

Workshop Agenda

4. Flash Your Creativity	Minutes 1 hr.	Start / Stop 4:00 / 5:00	Actual Start / Stop
Brainstorming	5	4:00 / 4:05	_____ / _____
What Can You Do?	20	4:05 / 4:25	_____ / _____
Lighting Others' Creativity	10	4:25 / 4:35	_____ / _____
Conclusion	25	4:35 / 5:00	_____ / _____

4. Flash Your Creativity (4:00 to 5:00)

00:05   **Brainstorming**

FACILITATOR COMMENTARY

REFER to the *Brainstorming* handout (p. 171-172) and overhead (p. 277).

SAY: A creativity training without brainstorming is like a:

_____.

(Have the participants fill in the blank as a reminder of the compare technique, e.g. "like a day without sunshine.")

I'm sure you've all been in brainstorming sessions in the past, but this will remind us of the guidelines that encourage a successful creative session.

Brainstorming has been around since advertising executive Alex Osborne introduced it in the 1930s. This page will serve as a resource to us now and in the future.

Let's practice brainstorming in the next activity.

00:20   **What Can You Do?**

GROUP ACTIVITY

SAY:

As we begin to wrap up our day of creativity, let's do what we can to capture everyone's ideas.

We spent time today looking at what the company could do to encourage more creativity in the future. Now let's look at what we as individuals can do.

Let's brainstorm a list of all the things we could each do to enhance our personal creative ability.

You can use the *What Can You Do?* (p. 173) handout to create ideas or make quick notes or doodle. Do not spend time writing all the ideas. We will have someone type them after this session.

ASK for two volunteers, one to facilitate the brainstorming session and the second to hang the flipchart pages on the wall as you fill them.

LIST the ideas on a flipchart page as fast as people say them. Allow about 15 minutes for the idea generation.

ASK for a volunteer to type and distribute them to the group.

00:10   **Lighting Others' Creativity**

FACILITATOR COMMENTARY

REFER to the *Lighting Others' Creativity* (pp. 174-175) handout. Have participants read the quotes and complete the questions.

ASK:

- Who would like to share your thoughts about this page?

- Who can you encourage to be more creative?

- Any ideas about how you might do that?

- Other thoughts?

Refer to the *Candle With Quote* overhead (p. 278).

SAY:

You have an opportunity to light others' creativity. You are both the candle and the mirror, able to light your own creativity and reflect the creativity of those you touch.

00:25   **Conclusion**

SAY:

You started today off in the dark. Hopefully you've been able to fan the sparks of creativity to begin to light your way. Sometimes intentions at the end of a session like this are great, but time passes and things that we must do get in the way of what we intended to do. The next activity will serve as a reminder several weeks down the road of what you intended to do.

Please turn to the *Creatively Yours* (p. 176) action plan page. Then, write a letter to yourself addressing:

- How you will be more creative.

- How you will help others be more creative.

- How you will ensure that the company has a creative climate.

Use the ideas that we all generated during the *Brainstorming* activity and *The Company's Creative Future* activity.

Place your letter to yourself in the envelope and address it. You will receive this reminder of your intentions in 4 to 5 weeks.

Collect the envelopes and send them to participants in 4 weeks.

ASK if anyone would like to share their plans. Point out that 90% of publicly stated goals are reached.

 REFER participants to the *Reading List* (p. 177) and suggest that if they would like to continue to learn more about the subject, these are some of the recommended books. Note that there is a mixture of creativity technique books as well as books that address creativity in business. For those new to creativity, recommend that they start with the Roger von Oech books.

 SAY:

It's been an exciting and enlightening day. We would like to capture some of your thoughts about the day on the *Session Evaluation* (p. 178). And, of course, if you'd like you may complete the evaluation with crayons. That seems like it might be fitting and appropriate.

Wait for them to complete the evaluation and as you see people wrapping up prepare to close the session.

 You will need to choose one of the three endings that seems most appropriate for this group.

Option 1:   *DISPLAY* the *Creative Flashes* overhead (p. 279) and *SAY*:

We started today in the dark, and we promised to provide you with techniques to ignite your creativity. We hope that we've made your world a bit more colorful and that you enjoyed yourself as you explored ways to widen your spectrum. Hopefully you have sparked your creativity and can now flash your creativity to others.

Option 2:   *DISPLAY* the *Come Out of Your Shell* overhead (p. 280) and *SAY:*

I hope you have enjoyed this session. May you widen your creative spectrum and come out of your creativity shell to see the light of creativity.

Option 3:   *DISPLAY* the *Flower* overhead (p. 281) and *SAY:*

I hope you have enjoyed this session. May you widen your creative spectrum beyond yellow flowers and green stems and see the light of creativity.

Chapter Four:

Half-Day Creativity Workshop

This chapter contains the training plan for your half-day creativity workshop. You may use it exactly as it is. It has been conducted dozens of times, so you can be assured that it works. Or you may tailor it to meet your needs. Chapter 2 provides tailoring suggestions.

> ### WHAT'S IN THIS CHAPTER?
>
> **This chapter focuses specifically on the half-day design. Its main focus is to prepare you for the workshop. In it you will find:**
>
> - **Purpose and objectives of the workshop.**
> - **Facilitator preparation.**
> - **Detailed half-day training design.**

This half-day workshop has been developed for any group of people who want to enhance their creative abilities. It is not as in-depth as the one-day workshop. It does not provide the hands-on practice skills for unboxing participants' creativity nor does it allow for practicing the ten creativity techniques. In addition, the *Light Your Company's Creativity* module has been eliminated. This means that this session takes a very personal (rather than corporate) approach.

If you have not yet done so, we recommend that you read Chapter 2 for a detailed description about how to prepare for facilitating a creativity session.

Workshop Purpose and Objectives

The overall purpose of this creativity workshop is to introduce participants to the concept of creativity. The half-day design provides an opportunity for participants to get in touch with their personal beliefs about creativity. It also presents ten creativity techniques.

As a result of this half-day session participants will be able to:

- Define creativity.

- Identify their personal creativity boxes.

- Design their individualized creative environment.

- Use a variety of creativity techniques to encourage creative efforts.

- Understand the relationship between taking risks and creativity.

- Relate creativity to the company's culture and future needs.

- Target personal goals to increase their creative efforts.

- Use creativity skills learned in the session on the job.

Facilitator Preparation

Recommended Number of Participants

Due to the high concentration of information in a short period of time, we recommend limiting the workshop to 15–18 people. Even with these numbers, balancing participation will be difficult.

Room Set-Up Suggestions

- Ideally, the training room should have no windows.

- At the minimum, you must be able to darken the room for the opening activity.

- Have training room arranged for small group work. (We suggest round tables or U-shape configuration.)

- Place a flashlight, set of participant materials and table tent at each participant's place.

- Set boxes of crayons and small cans of Play-Doh (about one of each for every three participants) on the training tables, spread out so that all participants can reach one or the other easily.

- Set up a toy table with toys of your choice and other sensory stimulating materials.

- We suggest that you play "mood" music quietly as participants enter the training room.

Workshop Agenda

1. **In the Dark**	Minutes 1 hr. 55	Start / Stop 8:00 / 9:55	Actual Start / Stop
Introduction	20	8:00 / 8:20	_____ / _____
Meet the Creative Me	20	8:20 / 8:40	_____ / _____
Objectives	5	8:40 / 8:45	_____ / _____
Can Creativity Be Defined?	20	8:45 / 9:05	_____ / _____
Do You Know. . . ?	20	9:05 / 9:25	_____ / _____
Toy Break	15	9:25 / 9:40	_____ / _____
Nine Uncreative Boxes	15	9:40 / 9:55	_____ / _____

2. **See the Light**	Minutes 1 hr.	Start / Stop 9:55 / 10:55	Actual Start / Stop
My Creative Climate	15	9:55 / 10:10	_____ / _____
A Spectrum of Creativity Techniques	35	10:10 / 10:45	_____ / _____
Out of Your Box Break	10	10:45 / 10:55	_____ / _____

3. **Flash Your Creativity**	Minutes 1 hr. 5	Start / Stop 10:55 / 12:00	Actual Start / Stop
Creative Spectrum Discussion	20	10:55 / 11:15	_____ / _____
Brainstorming	5	11:15 / 11:20	_____ / _____
What Can You Do?	20	11:20 / 11:40	_____ / _____
Conclusion	20	11:40 / 12:00	_____ / _____

Materials and Equipment Checklist

☐ Your facilitator notes.

☐ Participant materials.

☐ Name tents (p. 46).

☐ *Flash Your Creativity* flashlights (penlight flashlights—one each).

☐ Flipchart and pens to be used at your discretion.

☐ Overhead projector, screen and pens.

☐ Overhead transparencies.

☐ Audio cassette player, creativity-sparking musical tapes.

☐ Box of crayons for every 3 or 4 participants.

☐ Small can of Play-Doh for every 3 or 4 participants.

☐ A crisp one dollar bill and a quarter.

☐ Materials needed to stimulate senses as defined by you.

☐ Toys of your choice from your toy box.

☐ *Idea Sparker Cards* (if available; p. 291).

☐ Samples of kid's fun food (e.g., Pop Rocks, Cracker Jacks, Bazooka bubble gum).

☐ Group table tents (pp. 284-232).

☐ *Turtle Awards* (p. 289).

☐ Ink pads (and disposable towelettes for clean-up).

☐ *Road to Success Script* (pp. 225-232) and slides (if available; p. 292).

☐ Masking tape.

☐ Blank envelopes, one per participant.

☐ Materials for optional activities of your choice:

_____

_____

_____

Suggestions for Your "Toy Table"

- ☐ Coloring books.

- ☐ Play-Doh.

- ☐ Jump rope.

- ☐ Soft Frisbee.

- ☐ Kaleidoscopes.

- ☐ Yo-yo.

- ☐ Pickup sticks.

- ☐ Jacks.

- ☐ Nerf ball.

- ☐ Clay.

- ☐ Koosh ball.

- ☐ Puzzles.

- ☐ Paddle ball.

- ☐ Marbles.

- ☐ Juggling items.

- ☐ Prisms.

- ☐ Harmonica.

- ☐ Bubbles.

- ☐ Colored chalk.

- ☐ Kazoo.

- ☐ Crayons.
  (Especially the neon, glitter, metallic swirl, scented, fluorescent or any others that are new on the market.)

Participant Materials

The masters for all participant materials can be found in Chapter 6. You will need to make one handout for each participant. In addition, as mentioned in Chapter 2, you need to decide how to bind these materials. Since this session has quite a few handouts, you could consider a small three-ring binder or have them spiral bound. Another approach, less expensive and totally within your control is to use pocket folders. Divide the materials into their three modules and put a cover page on each (perhaps color coded). Then place all three smaller packets in a pocket folder.

- [ ] Cover Page (p. 135).

- [ ] Questioning Creativity? (pp. 136-137).

- [ ] Meet the Creative Me (p. 138).

- [ ] Can Creativity Be Defined? (p. 139).

- [ ] Do You Know. . . ? (p. 140).

- [ ] Nine Uncreative Boxes (p. 142).

- [ ] My Creative Climate (p. 149).

- [ ] A Spectrum of Creativity Techniques (p. 150).

- [ ] Brainstorming (pp. 171-172).

- [ ] What Can You Do? (p. 173).

- [ ] Creatively Yours (p. 176).

- [ ] Reading List (p. 177).

- [ ] Session Evaluation (p. 178).

Overhead Transparencies

You will need only ten of the overhead transparencies for this workshop. Make one of each. We recommend that you "make them colorful" in some way. You may simply color them with a permanent marker or add self-adhering colored film. They could also be scanned into your computer and computer colored. For a professional appearance, be sure to put them into transparency frames.

☐ Define Creativity (p. 265).

☐ Making of the New (p. 266).

☐ Discovery Consists (p. 269).

☐ Nine Uncreative Boxes (p. 270).

☐ Opportunityisnowhere (p. 271).

☐ Unbox Your Creativity (p. 272).

☐ A Spectrum of Creativity Techniques (p. 273).

☐ Brainstorming (p. 277).

☐ Creative Flashes (p. 279).

☐ Come Out of Your Shell (p. 280).

Flipcharts

The following flipcharts are used in this workshop:

Objectives

- Define Creativity.
- Identify creativity boxes.
- Design your creative environment.
- Use a variety of creativity techniques.
- Use creativity skills on the job.

Tasks for Your Creative Spectrum Discussion

- Identify two ways each technique could be used in your workplace.
- Identify two advantages of each technique.

A reminder

Creativity can be a threatening topic for some. Prepare yourself to teach this topic differently from any other. Because you'll be conducting unique activities that tap into a participant's right brain, it may take time for them to feel comfortable with your techniques. Therefore, you may observe discomfort, may need to wait longer for responses, may need to be prepared with starter responses, may need to justify an activity or may need to offer more reinforcement than usual.

Be persistent and patient and remain enthusiastic. They'll soon get into right-brain thinking and realize that they can learn while having fun. The better you prepare, the more successful you will be.

Training Plan

1. In the Dark

Purpose	The purpose of this module is to introduce some interesting facts about creativity and to push participants to right-brain thinking.
Materials needed	• Flashlights.
	• Name tents (p. 46).
	• Crayons.
	• Paper.
	• Dollar bill, quarter.
	• Group table tents (pp. 284-288).
	• Handout *Questioning Creativity* (pp. 136-137).
	• Handout *Meet the Creative Me* (p. 138).
	• Handout *Can Creativity Be Defined?* (p. 139).
	• Handout *Do You Know. . . ?* (p. 140).
	• Handout *Nine Uncreative Boxes* (p. 142).
	• Handouts *Unbox Your Creativity* (pp. 143-147).
	• Overhead *Define Creativity* (p. 265).
	• Overhead *Making of the New* (p. 266).
	• Overhead *Discovery Consists* (p. 269).
	• Overhead *Nine Uncreative Boxes* (p. 270).

Workshop Agenda

1. In the Dark	Minutes 1 hr. 55	Start / Stop 8:00 / 9:55	Actual Start / Stop
Introduction	20	8:00 / 8:20	_____ / _____
Meet the Creative Me	20	8:20 / 8:40	_____ / _____
Objectives	5	8:40 / 8:45	_____ / _____
Can Creativity Be Defined?	20	8:45 / 9:05	_____ / _____
Do You Know. . . ?	20	9:05 / 9:25	_____ / _____
Toy Break	15	9:25 / 9:40	_____ / _____
Nine Uncreative Boxes	15	9:40 / 9:55	_____ / _____

1. In the Dark (8:00 to 9:55)

FACILITATOR COMMENTARY

00:20

Introduction

Begin when all participants are seated and it's time to start the session. Softly start the mood music and turn on your flashlight. Then, turn off the room lights and begin the session in the dark.

 WELCOME participants to *Widen Your Spectrum.*

 SAY: You're about to enter a world of color and laughter; ideas and fun—your own private world of creativity, an experiment of YOU.

- Within each of us exists an infinite capacity for creating ideas and nurturing them to the point of innovation. Today you will explore how we, as individuals, have boxed ourselves in, prevented the flow of ideas, inhibited creativity and kept ourselves in the dark.

- You may choose to remain in the dark, or to ignite your creative spark. Today I challenge you to harness your creative energy as we explore numerous theory-based creativity techniques. You'll learn to focus your creativity. There is a ray of hope.

- Some of you have already begun to flash your creativity (if some participants have found and are using the flashlights). Take a few moments now to explore it more. You have a flashlight in front of you. Use it to be creative.

 WAIT for participants to use the flashlights.

Give the participants a moment to "be creative" with their flashlights. Some will not feel comfortable and ask questions. Just assure them they should be creative with their flashlights. Wait about 30 seconds to one minute, then continue talking.

DO NOT TURN ON THE LIGHTS YET!

 SAY:

Creativity doesn't just happen. It is not available on demand even though we are all born with creative potential.

The success of creativity is a learned process. You can transform your black and white thinking into colorful innovations.

Therefore, I challenge you to begin to widen and brighten your spectrum. Welcome to the colorful world of creativity!

Turn the *LIGHTS ON* and the *MUSIC OFF*.

ASK how many of the participants were uncomfortable while trying to be creative with the flashlights?

Expect that many are going to admit that they were uncomfortable. You might encounter strong resistance and negative comments to this activity (e.g., "It was too contrived," "It was hokey," "I don't see what it had to do with creativity"). Listen to such questions earnestly accepting the discomfort felt by the people giving the feedback. Do not avoid these issues—this is imperative to the success of the entire session. You must address them. The following will help you.

SAY:

The exercise was designed to be somewhat uncomfortable. The concepts of creativity are new to most people, and it's difficult to perform them "on demand."

Throughout the session you will encounter experiences that will take you farther and farther into your creative mode, or right brain. The session is loaded with creativity techniques. Traditional work and education stress the left brain skills (e.g., logic, math, organization, etc.). My job as facilitator is to push you as far right as you can go. New skills must be practiced.

The first handout, *Questioning Creativity?* (pp. 136-137), may address some of your issues. You may take a look at that later.

ASK: Why were they uncomfortable?

LISTEN for answers such as:

- It makes some feel different or foolish.

- Some will be lost because the instructions were so open-ended. We are used to getting detailed instructions.

- It was threatening, risky and scary to some. People fear the unknown; they fear failure.

SAY: All of these responses are the boxes we've put ourselves in which inhibit creativity.

Reinforce anyone who enjoyed the activity, yet be empathetic and understanding with those who didn't.

INTRODUCE yourself to the group.

SAY: We will take the next few minutes to meet one another.

00:20   **Meet the Creative Me**

GROUP ACTIVITY

 TELL each participant to complete the *Meet the Creative Me* (p. 138) handout. Model your answers to these questions to ease any discomfort they may have in opening up their creative side to the group. Use the sample answers provided in the Trainer's Notes, or better yet create your own.

 TELL participants to take four to five minutes to complete the page. Then have them use their answers to introduce themselves to the large group. We recommend that you start with random volunteers instead of the typical going around the table for two reasons:

- It's unique, creative, different from the typical—which allows you to model what this session is all about.

- If some people are feeling uncomfortable, they can volunteer when they feel more comfortable. Therefore, you are modeling adult learning theory practices—allowing people to feel in control of their environment.

ASK if anyone felt uncomfortable using this format for introductions. You may wish to discuss the following points:

- This was a right-brain way of introducing self.

- Some people feel uncomfortable using the right brain to reveal "self." They feel naked, unprotected.

ASK if anyone fell into the trap of working from the left-brain or logical side. Don't expect an answer to this particular question, but follow quickly asking for a show of hands to these questions:

How many of you felt:

- A need to go from top to bottom?

- A need to stick to a theme?

- There was a right or wrong answer?

- Your creativity would be judged?

- All the blanks had to be filled in?

- You had to finish?

ASK why they think this may have occurred.

98

REFER to the bottom of the handout and *ASK* for their thoughts about how the quotation by William James (1842–1910, psychologist and philosopher) relates to what just occurred. Use the discussion to illustrate these points:

- People can change.

- Our attitudes affect the way we behave.

- If we think we are something, then we will be just that.

 *ASK* what's the worst thing that can happen to you during this session? Expect answers such as:

- I will be asked to do something I cannot do.

- I will look stupid or foolish.

- I will be asked to do something I do not believe in.

- I will not be creative.

SAY in summary:

Creative people will be creative, no matter which job they perform. There is a company which has the following rule: "The only rule in this company is that there are no rules." In this session, there are no rules. Walk around when you like. Observe and try activities in the room at your leisure. Take breaks when you need them. Sit on the floor if you like. We are going to push your creativity to the limits at first. By the end of the session, you will be able to harness your creativity and use it more than you have in the past.

 REFER to the name tents activity portion of the *Meet the Creative Me* handout (p. 138) and have anyone who has not yet completed it do so now, making the following points:

- Print the names they wish to be called (yes, it could even be their new names from this exercise).

- They may decorate it with the crayons or markers or anything else they see around the room. Yours should be a model decorated with flowers, shapes, rainbows or whatever moves you.

- An optional, but fun, continuation of this project is to say that, in addition, they can put the name of their inner child on the inside of the table tent! Do this only if the group is ready for it!

Move on. Do not wait for participants to decorate their table tents. (A sample name tent appears on page 46.)

FACILITATOR COMMENTARY

00:05   **Objectives**

REFER to the flipchart listing the objectives of the session. They may be similar to the following. However, if you have customized the session in any way, be sure that they are all applicable. As a result of this half day session participants will be able to:

- Define creativity.

- Identify the boxes that prevent your personal creativity.

- Design your individualized creative environment.

- Use a variety of creativity techniques to encourage creative efforts.

- Understand the relationship between taking risks and creativity.

- Relate creativity to the company's culture and future needs.

- Encourage and support others' creative efforts.

- Use creativity skills learned in the session on the job.

POST the flipchart on the wall during the next break.

GROUP ACTIVITY

00:20   **Can Creativity Be Defined?**

TELL participants to break into groups according to height. Do not give any other instructions. Allow plenty of time for them to figure out what this means. Some may get hung up on "doing it right." Remind them, "No rules." We impose our own rules. There are many ways to break into groups "according to height." (e.g., line up and split into X groups; tall, average and short into three groups; one tall, one average and one short in each group; or anyway because we all "have height.")

SAY as a summary:

- This is another example of boxing ourselves in as we search for the rules.

- There are many "right ways to do things."

- The point is there is no "one correct way."

SAY, to introduce the activity:

Let's define creativity. We need to know it when we see it. In your groups, come up with a definition and a description or a symbol for creativity. Be prepared to share your ideas with the larger group and feel free to use the flipchart if you wish.

You may use the *Can Creativity Be Defined?* (p. 139) handout to record your ideas.

ASK representatives from the groups to share their ideas.

USE the overhead *Define Creativity* (p. 265) to record their responses.

SHARE the overhead *Making of the New* (p. 266), and say this is Mike Vance's (The Disney Corporation) definition.

Other definitions to guide the discussion are:

- The ability to bring about a new idea or invention.

- The ability to be original.

- The ability to bring something into being; give rise to.

REFER to the quotation at the bottom of the handout, "Everything that can be invented has been invented," by Charles H. Duell (Director of U.S. Patent Office, 1899).

SAY:

Duell's quotation is humorous, but he meant it most seriously. Compare what he is saying to, "There is nothing new under the sun," a quotation from the Bible, Ecclesiastes 1:9.

Point out that both quotations illustrate an important fact about creativity—it takes what is and makes it different to bring about a new idea or invention.

Notes

- _____
- _____
- _____
- _____
- _____
- _____
- _____
- _____
- _____
- _____
- _____
- _____
- _____
- _____

FACILITATOR COMMENTARY

00:20   **Do You Know. . . ?**

 Refer to the *Do You Know. . . ?* (p. 140) handout.

 SAY:

We have been exploring the nature of creativity, and this page provides lines for you to take notes as I review some interesting facts about creativity.

Using the Trainer's Notes for *Do You Know. . . ?* (p. 201-202), read each item in order (from top to bottom, starting with number 11) asking,
"Do you know. . ."

 ASK if they would like to discuss any of the points further.

 TELL participants to turn the page. If no one has asked about the numbering of questions—ask them why? The point to make is that we're often afraid to ask questions. We don't want to seem "stupid." Remember, there are no rules.

00:15   **Toy Break**

 Adult learning theory requires that participants are comfortable. You should encourage your participants to take informal breaks for any reason, at any time. However, you must still take formal breaks at least every 90 minutes. That time is now. Give participants a 15 minute break.

This break should be announced as a "toy break." Draw attention to the "toy table," a table on one side of the room where you have placed a variety of toys for the participants to play with.

The objectives are to:

* Help participants get in touch with their childhood, when they more than likely felt more free to be creative.

* Release the child that likes to play. Play leads to creativity.

* Encourage participants to get out of their boxes that prevent them from being creative.

For ideas, refer to *Suggestions for Your Toy Table* in Chapter 2.

REFER to the *Discovery Consists* overhead with the quote by Szent-Györgyi (p. 269) to bring people back from the break.

FACILITATOR COMMENTARY

00:15   **Nine Uncreative Boxes**

Refer to the Trainer's Notes for the activity, *Getting Out of the Box* (p. 205), for detailed instructions for this exercise.

ASK: Why aren't we more creative?

- We have routines that guide us and provide structure to operate on a daily basis. If we got up in the morning and tried to brainstorm 50 ways to cook an egg—we'd never get to work. We need routines.

- We have developed attitudes or "boxes" that trap our creativity. We create many of these for ourselves. We box ourselves in with these attitudes.

DEMONSTRATE the following example, as described in the Trainer's Notes.

Display a dollar bill and a quarter and ask one participant to balance the quarter on the edge of the dollar bill. Praise creative solutions to this problem. After several attempts, provide the solution.

Fold the dollar accordion style and lay the quarter on top. This is a simple example of how we are boxed in by questions and our paradigms.

REFER to the *Nine Uncreative Boxes* (p. 142) handout and the overhead, *Nine Uncreative Boxes* (p. 270). Use a pointer to focus participants' attention on each box as you speak about it.

SAY:

Just as we began our work together in the dark, there are nine boxes that we can allow ourselves to be locked within. The *Nine Uncreative Boxes* handout (p. 142) lists and illustrates these. Let's review them one by one. Color any of these that you feel box in your creativity.

- Use the definitions from the Trainer's Notes for *Getting Out of the Box* (pp. 206-207).

2. See the Light

Purpose

In this module, participants will examine their own creativity climate and will be introduced to ten creativity techniques.

Materials needed

- Handout *My Creative Climate* (p. 149).

- Handout *A Spectrum of Creativity Techniques* (p. 150).

- Trainer's Script *Ten Idea-Generating Techniques* (pp. 219-222).

- Overhead *A Spectrum of Creativity Techniques* (p. 273).

- Overhead *Opportunityisnowhere* (p. 271).

- Overhead *Unbox Your Creativity* (p. 272).

- Group table tents (pp. 284-288).

Workshop Agenda

2. See the Light	Minutes 1 hr.	Start / Stop 9:55 / 10:55	Actual Start / Stop
My Creative Climate	15	9:55 / 10:10	_____ / _____
A Spectrum of Creativity Techniques	35	10:10 / 10:45	_____ / _____
Out of Your Box Break	10	10:45 / 10:55	_____ / _____

2. See the Light (9:55 to 10:55)

FACILITATOR COMMENTARY

00:15   **My Creative Climate**

 SAY:

In part one of the session, we explored ways to break out of our uncreative boxes. Now, let's turn our attention to building the type of environment that encourages and rewards creative efforts.

Most creative people understand the need for a specific environment or routine that enhances their creative abilities. Some famous people have shared what "keeps their creative juice flowing."

For example:

- Mozart (18th–century Austrian composer) needed to exercise before he composed music.

- Dr. Samuel Johnson (18th–century English author) wanted a purring cat, orange peels and tea in his creative environment.

- Immanuel Kant (German philosopher) liked to work in bed at times with blankets arranged in a special way.

- Hart Crane (20th–century American poet) played jazz loudly on a Victrola.

- Johann Schiller (18th–century German poet) needed to fill his desk with rotten apples.

- Archimedes (ancient Greek mathematician and inventor) recognized the importance of relaxing and often solved his most difficult problems in a hot bath.

- Samuel Cray of super-computer fame, digs a tunnel beneath his house when he feels blocked from creative ideas.

Get in touch with what makes you feel creative. Is it certain scents (the change of seasons, cinnamon, baking bread), sights (sunrise, mountains, vacation pictures, flowers), sounds (ocean waves, jazz music, silence), tastes (chocolate, oranges, cappuccino) or feels (cool glass, comfortable sweatshirt, spring breeze)? What makes you feel more creative?

 REFER to the *My Creative Climate* handout (p. 149). Share your own creative climate needs as an example. Jot them down before the session.

TELL participants to:

 • Take five minutes to complete their *My Creative Climate* handout (p. 149).

 • Share ideas as a large group.

FACILITATOR COMMENTARY

00:35

A Spectrum of Creativity Techniques

 Refer to the *A Spectrum of Creativity Techniques* handout (p. 150) and overhead (p. 273). Use the revealing technique to uncover each technique as you speak about it. This will help your participants stay focused.

 SAY that as you briefly explain each of the techniques, you would like them to write a few notes. (See the Trainer's Script *Ten Idea Generating Techniques* on pages 219-222.)

• Compare and Combine.

• Risk Taking.

• Expand and Shrink.

• Ask, What's Good? and What If?

• Transform Your Viewpoint.

• In Another Sequence.

• Visit Other Places.

• Incubate.

• Trigger Concepts.

• Youth's Advantage.

Notes

• _____

• _____

• _____

• _____

• _____

• _____

• _____

• _____

• _____

• _____

INDIVIDUAL ACTIVITY

00:10   **Out of Your Box Break**

SAY that they will have a ten minute *Out of Your Box Break*. This can mean anything they wish it to mean!

- You will need to place the five *Group Table Tents* (pp. 284-288) out during the break in preparation for the next activity.

DISPLAY the overhead, *Opportunityisnowhere* (p. 271), to bring participants back from break.

ASK "What does this say?" and wait for their responses.

MAKE these points:

- Opportunity is "now here," though some of us may read it as "no where."

- You just have to see it that way. It's a matter of perception.

- Isn't it interesting that the exact same letters can mean the opposite, depending upon how we read it? Our view of creativity, work and life can be viewed in the same way!

SAY:

If you want to see something that will really boggle your mind, this diagram can be seen in four different formations. Display the overhead, *Unbox Your Creativity* (p. 272), and have participants list what they see (a cube with a smaller cube cut out; a cube with a small cube attached; a room with a box in the corner; a room with a cave-like cube room beyond). You may need to turn the transparency upside down so that the four formations can be seen by most people.

Notes

- _____
- _____
- _____
- _____
- _____
- _____
- _____

3. Flash Your Creativity

Purpose   In this module, participants will identify steps they can take to become more creative.

Materials needed

- Handout *Brainstorming* (pp. 171-172).
- Handout *What Can You Do?* (p. 173).
- Handout *Creatively Yours* (p. 176).
- Handout *Reading List* (p. 177).
- Handout *Session Evaluation* (p. 178).
- Overhead *Brainstorming* (p. 277).
- Overhead *Creative Flashes* (p. 279).
- Overhead *Come Out of Your Shell* (p. 280).
- Group table tents (pp. 284-288).
- Envelopes—one per particpant.

Workshop Agenda

3. Flash Your Creativity	Minutes 1 hr. 5	Start / Stop 10:55 / 12:00	Actual Start / Stop
Creative Spectrum Discussion	20	10:55 / 11:15	_____ / _____
Brainstorming	5	11:15 / 11:20	_____ / _____
What Can You Do?	20	11:20 / 11:40	_____ / _____
Conclusion	20	11:40 / 12:00	_____ / _____

3. Flash Your Creativity (10:55 to 12:00)

GROUP ACTIVITY

00:20   **Your Creative Spectrum Discussion**

 SAY:

You're going to work in a small group for the next 15 minutes. To get you into those groups we're going to refer to some creativity preferences.

There are five table tents (*Is a closet poet, Would like to write a book, Enjoys daydreaming, Likes to play with clay, Has painted a picture*) around the room. Select the area that most represents you and to go to that spot.

Once there are _____ people in a group, move to your second choice. Establish a maximum number in each group. (For example, if you have 15 people, you might say, "no more than three people in a group; after three people are in a group, move to your second choice.")

 ASSIGN two creativity techniques to each group. Tell them they have ten minutes and refer them to the flipchart where you have posted the following two tasks:

* Identify two ways each technique could be used in your workplace.

* Identify two advantages of each technique.

 MONITOR the groups:

Move from group to group making sure they each know what they are to do. Circulate a couple of times to answer questions or keep them on track.

ANNOUNCE when two minutes of their time is left so they can begin to wrap up.

 SAY:

Let's get back together as a large group to share ideas about how these techniques could be used.

ASK each group to report their ideas.

Watch the time closely to ensure that each team has time to report.

FACILITATOR COMMENTARY

00:05

Brainstorming

REFER to the *Brainstorming* handout (pp. 171-172) and overhead (p. 277).

SAY:

A creativity training without brainstorming is like a:

_____.

(Have the participants fill in the blank as a reminder of the Compare technique, e.g. "like a day without sunshine.")

I'm sure you've all been in brainstorming sessions in the past, but this will remind us of the guidelines that encourage a successful creative session.

Brainstorming has been around since advertising executive Alex Osborne introduced it in the 1930s. This page will serve as a resource to us now and in the future.

Let's practice brainstorming in the next activity.

GROUP ACTIVITY

00:20

What Can You Do?

SAY:

As we begin to wrap up our workshop on creativity, let's do what we can to capture everyone's ideas.

Now let's look at what we as individuals can do.

Let's brainstorm a list of all the things we could each do to enhance our personal creative ability.

You can use the *What Can You Do?* (p. 173) handout to create ideas or make quick notes or doodle. Do not spend time writing all the ideas. We will have someone type them after this session.

ASK for two volunteers, one to facilitate the brainstorming session and the second to hang the flipchart pages on the wall as you fill them.

List the ideas on a flipchart page as fast as people say them. Allow about 15 minutes for the idea generation.

ASK for a volunteer to get them typed and distributed to the group.

FACILITATOR COMMENTARY

00:20   **Conclusion**

SAY:

You started today off in the dark. Hopefully you've been able to fan the sparks of creativity to begin to light your way. Sometimes intentions at the end of a session like this are great, but time passes and things that we must do get in the way of what we intended to do. The next activity will serve as a reminder several weeks down the road of what you intended to do.

Please turn to the *Creatively Yours* (p. 176) action plan page. Then, write a letter to yourself addressing:

- How you will be more creative.
- How you will help others be more creative.
- How you will ensure that the company has a creative climate.

Use the ideas that we all generated during the *Brainstorming* activity.

Place your letter to yourself in the envelope and address it. You will receive this reminder of your intentions in four to five weeks. Collect the envelopes and send them to particpants in four weeks.

ASK if anyone would like to share their plans. Point out that 90% of publicly stated goals are reached.

REFER participants to the *Reading List* (p. 177) and suggest that if they would like to continue to learn more about the subject, these are some of the recommended books. Note that there is a mixture of creativity technique books as well as books that address creativity in business. For those new to creativity, recommend that they start with the Roger von Oech books.

SAY:

It's been an exciting and enlightening day. We would like to capture some of your thoughts about the day on the *Session Evaluation* (p. 178). And, of course, if you'd like you may complete the evaluation with crayons. That seems like it might be fitting and appropriate.

Wait for them to complete the evaluation and as you see people wrapping up prepare to close the session.

You will need to choose one of the two endings that seems most appropriate for this group.

Option 1:   Use the *Creative Flashes* overhead (p. 279).

SAY:

We started today in the dark, and we promised to provide you with techniques to ignite your creativity. We hope that we've made your world a bit more colorful and that you enjoyed yourself as you explored ways to widen your spectrum. Hopefully you have sparked your creativity and can now flash your creativity to others.

Option 2:   Use the *Come Out of Your Shell* overhead (p. 280).

SAY:

I hope you have enjoyed this session. May you widen your creative spectrum and come out of your creativity shell to see the light of creativity.

Notes
- _____
- _____
- _____
- _____
- _____
- _____
- _____
- _____
- _____
- _____
- _____
- _____
- _____
- _____
- _____
- _____

Chapter Five:

One-Hour Creativity Workshops

The one-hour workshops have been developed as enhancements to the one-day and half-day workshops. Most of the material is new or is presented in a different way.

These sessions work well as brown bag lunch topics, teasers for the one-day workshops, supplemental work, follow-up after the one-day workshop or conference topic presentations.

For additional one-hour sessions, you may build your own by pulling modules out of the one-day workshop.

WHAT'S IN THIS CHAPTER

This chapter is formatted somewhat differently. Each one-hour workshop becomes its own mini-chapter within the chapter. The one-hour workshops in this chapter are:

1. **A Taste of Creativity**
2. **So You Think You Have an Idea**
3. **Getting Unstuck**
4. **The Five–Step Creative Process**

To prepare you for each of the workshops you will find:

- Purpose and objectives of the workshop.
- Facilitator preparation.
- Detailed one-day training design.

If you have not yet done so, read Chapter 2 for a detailed description about how to prepare for facilitating a creativity session. It also provides you with suggestions for how to use the sourcebook effectively.

A Taste of Creativity

Purpose

This session provides an entertaining thematic way to introduce creativity. Participants will explore their beliefs about creativity and how their beliefs may have prevented them from being creative. Participants will have the opportunity to practice several creativity techniques, including youth's advantage, and compare and combine, using food as the focus.

Class size

10-12 participants.

Materials needed

You will need the following items to conduct this one-hour workshop:

- Kid-like food (e.g., Pop Rocks, Cracker Jacks, bubble gum), enough so everyone has 1-2 items.

- Tables for participants to write on. We recommend round tables or rectangular tables set in a U-shape.

- Boxes of crayons on the table, one for each person.

- Plain paper in stacks on the tables (3-4 sheets per person).

- Flipchart, colored markers and masking tape.

- Handout *My Creative Viewpoint* (p. 179).

- Handout *A Taste of Creativity: Definition* (p. 180).

- Overhead projector (optional).

- Overhead *Define Creativity* (p. 265).

- Overhead *Making of the New* (p. 266).

Workshop Agenda

1. A Taste of Creativity	Minutes 60	Actual Start / Stop	Media and Materials
Introduction	10	_____ / _____	Kid food
My Creative Viewpoint	20	_____ / _____	Handout
Define Creativity	15	_____ / _____	Overheads, Handout
Conclusion	15	_____ / _____	Flipchart

1. A Taste of Creativity

FACILITATOR COMMENTARY

00:10   **Introduction**

SAY: Let's take time getting to know each other.

Since the name of this workshop is *A Taste of Creativity*, we are going to use a food theme throughout.

You'll notice kid foods on the table, like Pop Rocks, Cracker Jacks, and bubble gum. Feel free to sample them whenever you choose.

One creativity technique, youth's advantage, reminds us that if we get in touch with the child inside and eliminate some of our fears and inhibitions, it is easier to be creative. So do what you must to open up and get in touch with your inner child. If bubble gum does it, great! The crayons on the table serve the same purpose and should be used when you feel the urge!

Please introduce yourself. Provide your name, department (or whatever else might be appropriate) and complete the statement:

If I were a food I'd be _____

because _____ .

(For example, my name is Burt and if I were a food I'd be an apple because apples are wholesome, basic and fruity.)

Facilitate the discussion as everyone introduces themselves.

SAY:

You just used another creativity technique. The combine technique forces two related or unrelated items together to reveal similarities and other possibilities.

GROUP ACTIVITY

00:20   **My Creative Viewpoint**

REFER participants to the handout, *My Creative Viewpoint* (p. 179), and have them take three to four minutes to complete it alone.

Once all have completed this page, ask participants to form triads and share answers to the statements.

CALL time after ten minutes and bring the group together to process the activity.

ASK the following if you need starter questions:

- When does most creativity occur for you? (Following question Q.)

- In question 13, how did you define "enjoy?"

  Rewards will be different for everyone. Some will be intrinsic such as, "feels good," "satisfaction," etc. For others it may be extrinsic rewards such as, "recognition," "money," etc. Point out that both types of rewards are important and necessary to successfully encourage creative endeavors.

- Do you think it is as possible to demotivate creativity as it is to encourage it? (Following question #.)

- What do you think Bucky Fuller meant when he said, "Everyone is born an inventor"? (Buckminster Fuller, 20th–century American engineer and inventor of the geodesic dome.)

  Fuller would probably say that we need to recognize that we are all creative—that we learn to suppress our creativity as we age.

- How about the numbering system? What do you think we are trying to prove?

GROUP ACTIVITY

00:15   **Define Creativity**

 INTRODUCE the activity by saying:

Let's define creativity. We need to know it when we see it. Working in pairs, come up with a definition for creativity. Be prepared to share your ideas with the larger group and feel free to use the flipchart if you wish.

 You may use the handout, *A Taste of Creativity: Definition* (p. 180), to record your ideas.

The first two questions will get you warmed up.

 You may use a flipchart page for the picture if you wish.

 ASK a representative from each group to share their ideas and their pictures and use the overhead, *Define Creativity* (p. 265), to record their responses.

SHARE the definition on the overhead, *Making of the New* (p. 266), and say this is Mike Vance's (Disney Corporation) definition.

Other definitions to guide the discussion are:

• The ability to bring about a new idea or invention.

• The ability to be original.

• The ability to bring something into being; give rise to.

GROUP DISCUSSION

00:15   **Conclusion**

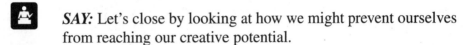 *SAY:* Let's close by looking at how we might prevent ourselves from reaching our creative potential.

WRITE on the flipchart:

Creativity is like a refrigerator because. . .

ASK the participants to complete the statement, "Creativity is like a refrigerator because. . .".

WRITE their ideas on the flipchart as they state them.

ALLOW about four minutes for this discussion.

SAY:

You have just used another creativity technique. It is the compare technique which demonstrates that if you use symbols, analogies, similes or metaphors to question assumptions, you will break through paradigms that you may have, thus opening up room for new ideas.

Let's use the final ten minutes to identify barriers or blocks that we may have to creativity and ways to break through them.

One person will state a barrier or block. Then we as a group must come up with two ways to break through it.

All ideas are correct.

Let's see if we can complete at least ten before we end the session.

To end the session, *SAY:*

I hope this taste of creativity has whet your appetite for more.

So You Think You Have an Idea. . .

Purpose   This session provides an opportunity for participants to discuss a new idea in a safe environment. Participants will discuss their ideas openly, while exploring the benefits, pitfalls and excitement of the idea, and develop plans for their next steps.

Class size   10-12 participants.

Materials needed   You will need the following items to conduct this one-hour workshop:

- Boxes of crayons on the table, one for each person.

- Flipchart, colored markers, masking tape.

- Handout *So You Think You Have an Idea. . .* (p. 181).

- Handout *From Here to There* (p. 182).

- Handout *What's Next?* (p. 183).

- Suggested Books for display:

  So You've Got a Great Idea by Steve Fiffer

  The Care & Feeding of Ideas by James Adams

  Six Thinking Hats by Edward de Bono

  Thinkertoys by Michael Michalko

  301 Great Management Ideas from America's Most Innovative Small Companies by Sara Noble

  A Whack on the Side of the Head by Roger von Oech

  Wake Up Your Creative Genius by Kurt Hanks and Jay Parry

  Why Didn't I Think of That? by Roger L. Firestien

  Thunderbolt Thinking by Grace McGartland

  99% Inspiration by Bryan W. Mattimore

  101 Creative Problem Solving Techniques by James M. Higgins

Workshop Agenda

2. So You Think You Have an Idea. . .	Minutes 60	Actual Start / Stop	Media and Materials
Introduction	10	_____ / _____	
My Newest Idea	25	_____ / _____	Flipchart, Handout
From Here to There	20	_____ / _____	Book selection, Handout
Conclusion	5	_____ / _____	Handout

2. So You Think You Have an Idea. . .

FACILITATOR COMMENTARY

00:10   **Introduction**

Begin by welcoming the participants.

 ASK: How many of you have ever had a good idea?

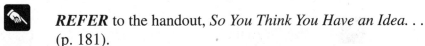 *SAY:* Let's hear about them.

Introduce yourself. Provide your name, department (or whatever is appropriate) and tell us about the best idea you ever had.
(Go around to everyone.)

Now I'm assuming most of you are here because you have another good idea. So let's get to them.

00:25   **My Newest Idea**

 REFER to the handout, *So You Think You Have an Idea. . .*
(p. 181).

 SAY: Take five minutes to complete this page as an individual.

CALL time after five minutes.

GROUP ACTIVITY

SAY: Now find a partner. The two of you will become each other's "Idea Coach."

POST the following job description of the "Idea Coach" on the flipchart:

- Good listener.
- Asks questions to push for more creativity.
- Is positive. Can always find the "what's good about it."
- Supports even when the other is down.
- Is a spontaneous, creative, original thinker.

SAY:

All of you have the ability to do all of these. You just need to remember them when you are in the "Idea Coach" role.

Now look around the room to find someone with whom you can work today and also easily connect with after this session is over. Find that person now.

Take the next fifteen minutes (seven minutes for each of you plus one minute transition time) and explain your idea to the other person.

Remember, when you are the "Idea Coach," practice the five skills posted on the flipchart.

 ASK each "Idea Coach" to briefly describe, in two sentences, the other person's idea.

GROUP ACTIVITY

00:20   **From Here to There**

 REFER to the handout, *From Here to There* (p. 182), and have the pairs spend twenty minutes (ten minutes for each person's idea) completing it. The "Idea Coach" should make suggestions, ask questions, reinforce ideas and encourage the idea forward.

 SAY:

Go through each of the questions and complete what you can.

If you have time, I have brought in some books. You may consider checking them out to continue your search for how to make your idea a reality. There is room at the bottom of the page to list any books that interest you. Let me know if I can help you in any way.

Circulate among the pairs to ensure that they understand the task.

GROUP DISCUSSION

00:05   **Conclusion**

 SAY:

To close this session, let's each state one thing you are going to do when you leave this session. (Go around the group.)

I want to leave you with one message.

 REFER to the *What's Next?* (p. 183) handout.

 ASK: Get the message?

Getting Unstuck

Purpose	This session provides participants with an opportunity to learn and practice a brainstorming adaptation using four creativity techniques while generating a list of 400 ways to spark creativity.
Class set-up	10-12 participants.
	Due to the first activity, we recommend rectangular tables set in a U-shape.
Materials needed	You will need the following items to conduct this one-hour workshop:

- Boxes of crayons on the table, one for each person.

   (Get the most creative crayons you can find: the neon, glitter, metallic swirl, scented, fluorescent, or any others that are new on the market!)

- Creativity enhancing items on the tables.

   (e.g., Play-Doh, Koosh balls, clay, prisms, bubbles, Silly Putty.)

- Three flipcharts.

- Colored markers and masking tape.

- 400 index cards—a stack of 20 placed in front of each person.

- Dictionary.

- Handout *Brainstorming* (pp. 171-172).

- Handout *Getting Unstuck* (pp. 184-186).

Workshop Agenda

3. **Getting Unstuck**	Minutes 60	Actual Start / Stop	Media and Materials
Introduction	5	_____ / _____	Toys
Brainstorming	10	_____ / _____	Handout
Add an Idea	20	_____ / _____	Flipchart, Index cards
Small Group Generating	22	_____ / _____	Dictionary, Flipcharts
Conclusion	3	_____ / _____	Handout

3. Getting Unstuck

FACILITATOR COMMENTARY

00:05   **Introduction**

SAY: Welcome to all of you!

Today is an experiment to see if we can use the techniques we are here to learn to identify the techniques we need to learn.

Sound confusing? Hang in there.

We all need to use our creative potential, yet there are times when we all block and "can't think of a thing!" Today we are going to examine how we can get unblocked—unstuck. How can we spark creativity?

We'll practice a couple of techniques to generate ideas. The ideas we will be generating are those to—you guessed it—get unstuck!

The crayons, Play-Doh and other items on the table should be seen as creativity enhancing items that you should use whenever you feel the urge.

Let's introduce ourselves. Please give us your name, department (or other relevant information) and one thing that causes you to block on creating new ideas.

Now our challenge for today is to generate 400 ideas for getting unstuck. So we'd better get started!

00:10   **Brainstorming**

REFER to the handout, *Brainstorming* (pp. 171-172).

SAY:

A creativity training without brainstorming is like a

_____ .

(Have the participants fill in the blank.)

This is the compare creativity technique, e.g. "like a day without sunshine."

SAY:

I'm sure you've all been in brainstorming sessions in the past, but this will remind us of the guidelines that encourage a successful creative session.

Brainstorming has been around since advertising executive Alex Osborne introduced it in the 1930s. This page will serve as a resource to use now and in the future.

ASK: What are the key things we should remember when brainstorming? (Touch on each of the nine items on the first page.)

SAY: Let's practice brainstorming in the next activity, but we're going to give it a new twist and call it *Add an Idea*.

GROUP ACTIVITY

00:20   **Add an Idea**

SAY:

Let's begin generating our 400 ideas for how to trigger creativity. *Add an Idea* is an adaptation of brainstorming.

You have a stack of index cards in front of you. You will write one idea for how to spark creativity on a card.

The activity will be conducted in silence.

After you write your idea, you will pass it to your left. You will get a card from your right, read it, write another idea and then pass two cards to your left.

You will now get two cards, read them both, write a third card and pass all three.

This will continue until one entire circuit has been completed (ten people means ten rounds).

There is one difference from brainstorming. You can see that the ideas must be kept moving around the table. Therefore, if you can't think of an idea, write a question and people may begin to answer it. For example, you might ask, "what if you don't have time to be creative?" Some people may choose to answer that question, but many may not. The idea is to just keep things moving.

ASK: Are there any questions? Remember, we are looking for ways to spark creativity when you are blocked.

You will need to ensure that the activity continues to move quickly. If you run short of time because you have a large group or people are taking more time than usual, you may need to end it before one complete round.

SAY: Let's get some of the best ideas posted.

Would someone assist me by writing on the second flipchart? We will each write every other idea so that we can get them up faster.

Look at the stack of ideas you have, and choose the two that you like the best (they could be unique, fun, crazy, practical, work-able—the criteria doesn't matter at this point).

Do not post all the ideas, just get a sample up. Most of them have read many of them already. Inform them that they will get a complete list of all ideas from the session.

Hang these flipcharts on the walls during the next activity; don't take time from the session now.

Collect the index cards for typing later.

GROUP ACTIVITY

00:22   **Small Group Generating**

SAY:

We have generated _____ ideas; we still have _____ to go.

Let's form three small groups and each of those groups will focus on one particular area. And for fun let's have you name your team.

To form your team, count off backwards by 3's (3,2,1,3,2,1,3,2. . .).

Now, get into your teams and take two minutes to name your team (e.g., The Daydreamers, 400 or Bust, Idea Generators, Ideamakers). Take care that they do not get stuck on naming their team—two minutes is a maximum!

Each team will have separate instructions. Verbal instructions usually work, although you may wish to write them on a flipchart page or index cards for each team.

SAY: (substituting the team's name if they chose one)

Team A: You will use this dictionary. Have someone blindly point to a word and name it. Then the team generates ideas of how it makes you think of ways to spark creativity. Someone can list them on the flipchart next to your team. When the flow of ideas slows, point to another word. Your challenge is to get 100 ideas in the next fifteen minutes. (Trigger concept technique.)

Team B: You will focus on the five senses: sight, smell, hearing, touch and taste. How can your senses be stimulated to generate ideas? List at least 100 things on your flipchart in the next fifteen minutes. (Combine technique.)

Team C: You will have two areas:

- The first is to list all the places you could go to get creative ideas. Hint: don't let the physical word "go" inhibit you; you can go to an art gallery or the mall, but you could also go to a magazine. (Visit other places technique.)

- The second is to list how others would stimulate their creativity. Hint: don't limit yourselves to only people who are alive—like your child, a librarian, and co-workers. Ask how would Plato, George Washington, Archie Bunker, Mickey Mouse or Lassie get themselves unstuck? You have fifteen minutes to generate over 100 ideas on your flipchart. (Transform your viewpoint technique.)

 ASK the teams to present three of their favorite ideas.

FACILITATOR COMMENTARY

00:03   **Conclusion**

 SAY:

I believe we have met our challenge and have generated _____ ideas for getting you unstuck.

 ASK:

Do we have a volunteer who will type our ideas after the session and send a copy to me for the rest of the group?

As if we didn't generate enough ideas, let me give you a handout called *Getting Unstuck* (pp. 184-186). You may use it until we get our list typed and sent to you. (Be sure that you do not provide this handout before the teams generate their ideas.)

 SAY: Thanks for your participation and keep those ideas flowing!

If you send a copy of your ideas to the author, we will compile all the ideas and send you the complete set after one year. Send the list your group generated to Elaine Biech, ebb associates, Box 657, Portage, WI 53901.

The Creativity Process

Purpose	This session provides an opportunity to explore in depth the process that leads to creative ideas. Participants will identify the five–step creative process, and work on actual problems they bring to the workshop.
Class set-up	12-16 participants.
	Participants will need tables so that they can write. We recommend round tables or rectangular tables set in a U-shape.
Preparation	Participants should come to the session prepared to discuss a project, idea or problem they would like to explore using the creative process.
Materials needed	You will need the following items to conduct this one-hour workshop:

- Boxes of crayons on the table, one for every 3–4 participants.
- Overhead projector.
- Handout *The Five R's of Creativity* (p. 187).
- Handout *Steps in the Creative Process* (pp. 188-189).
- Overhead *The Five R's of Creativity (blank)* (p. 282).
- Overhead *The Five R's of Creativity (completed)* (p. 283).

Workshop Agenda

4. The Creativity Process	Minutes 60	Actual Start / Stop	Media and Materials
Introduction	5	_____ / _____	
Five R's of Creativity	50	_____ / _____	Overheads
Conclusion	5	_____ / _____	Overhead

4. The Creativity Process

FACILITATOR COMMENTARY

00:05   **Introduction**

Begin by welcoming participants to the workshop.

 SAY that they are here to explore their creativity for an hour.

 ASK: What comes to mind when I say the word "creativity?"

> (Expect to hear things such as "magic," "voodoo," "ideas," "spark," "new.")

 SAY:

Those may all be a part of creativity, but creativity, is also a process. A process that you can follow and use successfully, just like any process you use on the job. Let's examine that process now.

(If participants need introductions, you may add them at this point.)

GROUP ACTIVITY

00:50   **Five R's of Creativity**

 REFER participants to the handout (p. 187) and the blank overhead (p. 282) for *The Five R's of Creativity*.

 SAY:

Creativity does not happen magically; it is the result of a process—a system of thinking. There are five steps in the creative process. Just as there are the three R's of education, (reading, 'riting and 'rithmetic) each step in the creative process starts with the letter "R".

 ARRANGE yourselves in trios. In your groups, work together to number in sequence the *The Five R's of Creativity*. Then connect the numbers in sequence to uncover their pattern.

Observe the groups' progress as you walk around the room. Help out when needed. Once the groups have completed the activity, let them know that each of these steps will be explored in detail.

 REFER to the completed overhead, *The Five R's of Creativity* (p. 283) to illustrate the pattern.

 ASK if they believe that the shape is significant?

Some participants will arrive at the sequence creatively, by connecting the points first. Praise this as creativity. Remember, there are no rules in creativity.

GROUP DISCUSSION

 DISCUSS the quotation found at the bottom, "Ruth made a big mistake when he gave up pitching." (Tris Speaker speaking about Babe Ruth, 1921; American baseball player in the Hall of Fame, batting average of .344.)

 SAY:

Please turn to the *Steps in the Creative Process* (pp. 188-189) handout and let's begin to work through the five–step process using the situation that you were asked to bring to this workshop.

REFER to number 1, realize the need.

ASK what they think it means?

SAY:

Many creative ideas, projects and products were not "needed" until "discovered." For instance, some came about as mistakes (e.g., Post-it Notes). Others were found accidentally (e.g., penicillin.)

Some came at odd times (e.g., at breakfast a waffle became the model for the Nike shoe sole).

ASK: Do you know of any other accidental discovery stories?

GROUP ACTIVITY

 SAY:

Using the problem that you brought to the session, create a specific objective that summarizes what the result should be. Be prepared to share your objective with the larger group. Get feedback from the other two people in your trio.

You will have five minutes to write your objective statement.

ASK them to share their objectives and close this activity by making these points about the objectives:

1. They must be stated clearly and specifically.

2. They must be measurable.

3. They must meet the need.

SAY:

The second step in the creative process is to review all of the data available to you.

 Read the introductory remarks to step 2 and complete this activity individually.

We must continue to put information into our brain. We can organize it and arrange it later.

 GIVE them time to complete this step and have several share their resources and sources. Close by adding any unmentioned resources that you have noted for your company.

 SAY:

Once you have thoroughly reviewed the data, you need to let it rest. The third step in the creative process is to rest the data.

Lead a discussion around step 3 and add the following information on dreaming:

1. Keep pen and paper by your bed with light available.
2. Record your dreams, looking for patterns and re-occurrences.
3. Place a tape recorder by your bed.
4. Just before falling asleep, give yourself a mental suggestion that you will remember what you dream.
5. Before sleeping, think of a problem as a metaphor. The subconscious "likes" metaphors. Ask your subconscious for a solution.
6. If you talk in your sleep have someone awaken you.

 ASK for a volunteer to share an instance where resting the data or dreaming on it paid off. Be prepared to offer your own example.

 SAY:

If you have performed steps 1, 2 and 3, the 4th step will come on its own. Be prepared to recognize and capture the spark or idea or inspiration, or whatever you call the creative moment, when it hits you.

 REVIEW the introductory remarks for step 4 and have them complete the activity in their trios.

PROCESS this activity. Use a round robin to have them share their methods for capturing ideas with the larger group.

Be prepared to add onto their lists with these: a running note pad, taking notes while reading; person to awaken you if you talk in your sleep; repeating the information three times; reviewing notes daily; using association with objects or words; telling another person; and those methods that are unique to your organization (e.g., dictation available 24 hours by phone, hand-held Dictaphone, use of personal computers at work and at home).

 SAY:

The last step in the creative process is to refine. If you do not perform this last step, your creative spark may die out from lack of polishing.

 READ the introductory remarks for step 5 and review the JUDGE process by making these points:

J Justify

Justify its existence (positives). List all of the good things about your idea. Why is it good? What good will it create?

U Undermine

Undermine its development (negatives). Now, list all of the reasons why your idea will not work. Play your own devil's advocate.

D Delay

Delay your personal biases and attitudes (be neutral). Keep yourself from judging the idea too quickly. Stop yourself from making a decision at this time. Do not be hasty.

G Generate

Generate the decision (use a process). Use a decision-making tool that has worked for you in the past. (Be prepared to insert information on the specific kinds of decision-making tools and processes that are used at your company. You may discuss consensus, expert, authority rule with discussion, majority vote, minority control or any other decision-making methods that will be familiar to the participants. What about a coin toss?)

E Execute

Execute your decision (action). Do it! Ideas are worthless on the drawing board. Plan for the budget, anticipate objections, draw up a schedule, prepare an action plan and determine a contingency plan.

SAY:

Work in your trios to JUDGE the idea: Winning is everything.

When they have completed the activity, *ASK* for the results from each group.

00:05   **Conclusion**

SAY:

We've reached the end of this workshop, and I hope you have some ideas in general about how to use the five–step creative process as well as an idea or two about how your specific situation could be improved with creativity.

Let's close with several comments about what you learned today.

Have volunteers share ideas.

Notes

- _____
- _____
- _____
- _____
- _____
- _____
- _____
- _____
- _____
- _____
- _____
- _____
- _____
- _____
- _____
- _____
- _____
- _____

Chapter Six:

Participant Handouts

This sourcebook provides you with all the participant handouts you will need for all of the sessions. Of course, you are always encouraged to tailor, customize or develop your own.

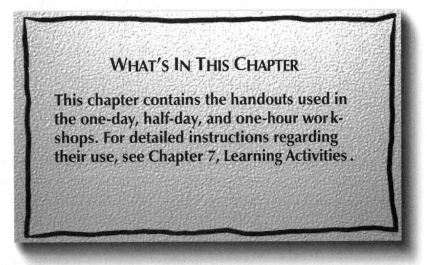

WHAT'S IN THIS CHAPTER

This chapter contains the handouts used in the one-day, half-day, and one-hour workshops. For detailed instructions regarding their use, see Chapter 7, Learning Activities.

The quotes and graphics have been added to stimulate creativity in general and discussion more specifically. In several places within the workshop we suggest that you ask about the quote or the graphic. Do this as often as you choose. Indeed, you could probably conduct an entire workshop around the quotes and graphics alone!

Do review all of the handouts before you facilitate the workshop for the first time. It's probably a good idea to actually complete the activities so that you know how you would respond to the requests you will make of the participants.

Most of the handouts are used in the one-day workshop. There are no new handouts in the half-day workshop (since it is a condensed version of the one-day workshop). However, new handouts are introduced in the one-hour workshops.

What Do You Do?

Once you know which workshop you're going to conduct, copy the appropriate handouts.

The list of participant materials can be found at the beginning of each workshop chapter. You will need to make one handout for each participant. In addition, as mentioned in Chapter 2, you need to decide how to bind these materials.

Since the one-day workshop has many pages, you may consider a small three-ring binder or have them spiral bound. Another approach, less expensive and totally within your control is to use pocket folders. Divide the materials into their four modules and put a cover page on each (perhaps color coded). Then place all four smaller packets in a pocket folder.

It is perfectly appropriate for the shorter sessions to simply collate the pages and staple them in the upper left-hand corner. If you wish to provide something that looks more permanent and professional, put the packets in a pocket folder.

By the way, you may also choose to use some of these materials to supplement other workshops you conduct. The *Brainstorming* handout, for example, could be used during a problem solving workshop, a process improvement workshop or a facilitator skills workshop.

One last creative, yet practical idea. Probably one of the most important handouts is *A Spectrum of Creativity Techniques*. Since it is important, has a light bulb graphic and suggests "bright ideas," we like to run it on bright yellow. No, not, pale pastel washed-out yellow. Bright! Jubilant! Exciting! Electrifying Yellow. Our favorite is a color called Astrobrights Solar Yellow. When all the other pages are white, it stands out—brightly!

Sample Cover Page

The facing page can be photocopied onto card stock and used as a cover page for your packets of participant materials.

Creativity

widen
your
spectrum

Questioning Creativity?

As you walked into this creativity session, what were you thinking? Did you wonder why you were here? Did you try to get a final grasp on just what creativity is before someone asked you? Were you thinking that the company really did it this time—paid for some far-out program that will waste your time? Everyone knows there are only a few creative people, and they're weird! If these, or other related thoughts, were popping into your mind, feel at ease. You're not alone. Such speculation and skepticism are normal reactions to a program about creativity.

Creativity Can Be a Scary Topic

Just what is it? Simply put, creativity is a process of taking information or material and rearranging it to form (create) a new entity or idea. That's all. There's nothing magical about it. Since it is a process, it can be learned. The steps and tools of creativity can be used by anyone.

Most companies are going through many changes. Many have recently invested in state-of-the-art technology. Many have plans to broaden their customer base. Some have redesigned the business processes by which they operate. Companies have flattened, de-layered, teamed, reengineered, process improved and reorganized.

Companies Are Changing

These changes create a new set of problems. Problems that require a new way of thinking: creativity to spawn the idea and risk taking to push the idea to an innovative result.

It seems like all companies have gone mad! Why? Companies must become more competitive. How? To increase the competitive advantage, companies can:

- Decrease costs.

- Increase quality.

- Increase speed.

- Master innovation.

The changes implemented by companies may accomplish the first three, but not the last. In addition, most companies are experiencing less than half their potential if the new workplace does not encourage creativity and reward risk. What are the new ways of thinking?

Questioning Creativity (cont.)

New Ways of Thinking

- **Innovation**

  Dramatic change occurring as a result of risking a new, creative idea.

- **Creativity**

  Mike Vance of the Disney Corporation says creativity is, "the making of the new and the rearranging of the old."

- **Risk Taking**

  Becoming vulnerable or exposed to possible loss or danger.

Creativity training has been used in the United States for over three decades. The incidence of such training has increased rapidly over the past few years. Why? Creativity helps conquer the challenges of change. Creativity forces you to view things in new ways. Human beings are the only resources capable of such diversified and complex thought processes.

Now, back to those questions you may have had. You're involved in this program because the company is providing you with the skills and tools necessary for generating creative ideas. The company is investing in you so that you and your co-workers can better conquer today's challenges with creativity. Everyone has the potential to be more creative. You, too. Glad you're here! Thanks for asking.

> "Indeed, without sufficient flexibility to permit random creativity in unexpected—and nonpreferred—places in the organization, many companies would not have developed new programs, new products, or new systems. . ."
>
> —Rosabeth Moss Kanter

Meet the Creative Me

Create a new identity for yourself in this program. Use the following outline to describe this creative you and put your new name on the name tent provided.

My name is: _____

I am a(n): _____

Using the five senses, I would describe myself as:

    I look like: _____

    I smell like: _____

    I feel like: _____

    I sound like: _____

    I taste like: _____

My latest adventure was:

_____

_____

_____

_____

_____

_____

_____

_____

> *"Human beings can alter their lives by altering their attitudes of mind."*
>
> —William James

Can Creativity Be Defined?

Definition:

Description:

creativity looks like ———————————————.
creativity tastes like ————————————————.
Creativity feels like ——————————————.
Creativity smells like ——————————————.
Creativity sounds like ——————————————.

Symbol:

"Everything that can be invented
has been invented."

—Charles H. Duell
Director of U.S. Patent Office, 1899

Do You Know. . . ?

11. That 86% of success in business at any level is dependent upon
_____ ?

8. That creativity and IQ _____ ?

2. That the supply of scientific information grows over 15% each
year, and that by the year 2000 this could jump to _____ ?

5. That Coca-Cola was originally invented as a _____ ?

4. That the Nike shoe sole design was patterned after
_____ ?

7. That most people use only _____ % of their total brain power ?

6. That people spend _____ % of their lives sleeping ?

3. That the purpose of the court jester in the Middle Ages was to
_____ ?

1. That by the age of seven,
most children are
using about _____ %
of their creative ability?

10. That creativity
can be learned?

9. That by the age of forty,
adults are about _____ %
as creative as they were
at seven?

Right-Brain/Left-Brain?

TIMELESS INTUITIVE VERBAL

VISUAL ANALYTICAL

SUBJECTIVE SEQUENTIAL

$E=Mc^2$

$2y+3x=4z$

OBJECTIVE

SPONTANEOUS CAUSE & EFFECT

SCIENCE & MATH

ARTS & MUSIC EMOTIONAL LOGICAL

"Who the hell wants to hear
actors talk?"

—Harry M. Warner
Warner Bros. Pictures, c. 1927

Nine Uncreative Boxes

Time Trapped
"I don't have time to be creative."

Risky Business Zone
"Being creative results in unsound, weird ideas"

Environmental Pollution
"I do not work in a creative environment."

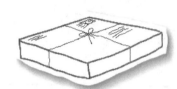

Perfectionist Problem
"I don't like to make mistakes."

Wright or Wrong Thinking
"I deal in wright and wrong."

Calm Waters
"Creativity can rock the boat."

Self-Fulfilling Prophecy
"I'm just not a creative person."

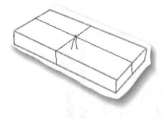

Bottom-Line Thinking
"Creativity wastes money."

Only One Right Answer
"Creativity generates too many options."

Unbox Your Creativity—A

Tear Apart Time Trapped Boxes!

To get out of the time trapped box, think of 21 instances in your daily routine when you can steal five minutes for creativity (e.g. while showering):

1.	8.	15.
2.	9.	16.
3.	10.	17.
4.	11.	18.
5.	12.	19.
6.	13.	20.
7.	14.	21.

Rip the Risky Business Zone!

To rephrase an old saying, " 'Tis better to have risked and lost than never to have risked at all." Children take risks constantly—in time we learn to be cautious. There is safety in being careful. This lesson is basic to survival. However, when it is carried too far, it can cause the death of our creativity. Adults can unlearn overly cautious behaviors and learn to take, and yes, even enjoy risks.

When was the last time you took a risk?

Are you a risk taker? Why or why not?

"There is no likelihood man can ever tap the power of the atom."

—Robert Millkan
Nobel Prize in Physics, 1923

Unbox Your Creativity—B

Perforate the Perfectionist's Problem!

School systems and society reward winning. Our athletic endeavors are based on W-I-N-N-I-N-G. Our whole environment breeds perfectionists, and many top-level people are plagued by this problem. Perfectionism isn't a gift—it's a curse. The one sure way to be a complete failure is to behave like a perfectionist. No human being can be perfect. Our role is to perfect. Use it as a verb:

P

E **Pinpoint your goal!**

R **Examine alternatives!**

F **Reach out for it!**

E **Feel it! Does it feel right?**

C **Evaluate your progress!**

T **Congratulate your effort!**

Try again!

Create positive bits of wisdom for the following:

1. To try is: _____

_____

2. Making a mistake is: _____

_____

3. Falling short of the goal: _____

_____

Unbox Your Creativity—C

End Wright or Wrong Thinking!

Black is black; white is white. Wright or wrong thinking leads to dead-end thoughts. It's either-or, from one end of a continuum to another. It's right or wrong. If you find yourself locked into this box, you need to learn to feel comfortable with the uncertain and the unknown. End wright or wrong thinking by exploring the "what if's."

Think of something you disagree with at work. Now list three "what if" questions that might move you to the middle of the continuum.

Empty the Self-Fulfilling Prophesy!

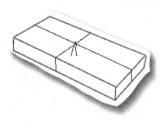

You are what you think. If you've had the habit of saying, "I'm not very creative," stop it immediately! Next time, say "I am very creative." Everyone is. Not everyone uses this ability. Take the next few minutes to take stock of your creative endeavors.

At home, I've been creative by:

At work, I've been creative by:

Unbox Your Creativity—D

Bust Bottom-Line Thinking!

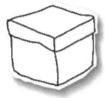

Bottom-line thinking is concerned with money. It views the creative process as wasteful. Thoughts such as "that's not logical," "keep your nose to the grindstone," and "that's not in my job description" can squash creative ideas. Without innovative, creative ideas, businesses will not be able to compete in today's market place. Innovations are those creative projects that meet your consumer's and customer's needs. Bust bottom-line thoughts by rephrasing them for innovation.

"That's not logical": _____

_____

"Keep your nose to the grindstone": _____

_____

"That's not in my job description": _____

_____

Pull Apart Environmental Pollution!

If you've been using your environment as an excuse to avoid being creative, you're fooling yourself. Sure, some outside influences do help foster and support creative ideas, but creativity is generated from within. Identify environmental excuses and devise solutions to overcome them on your own, without changing the environment.

Excuses   **Solutions**

Unbox Your Creativity—E

Eliminate Only One Right Answer!

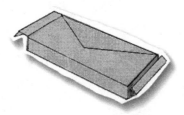

If you find only one right answer, it's because you stopped looking. Think about it. . . . Now, find other right answers.

You need more money. You decide to get a weekend job. That's your first right answer. Think of seven more:

1.

2.

3.

4.

5.

6.

7.

Ripple Calm Waters!

Many people feel trapped within this box— "don't rock the boat." Calm waters should be rippled in two instances: out-moded rules and new challenges. Under each category, list any ideas that may need to be rippled in your area.

Out-Moded Rules   **New Challenges**

Idea Sparker

Name 19 shades of green.

1.

2.

3.

4.

5.

6.

7.

8.

9.

10.

11.

12.

13.

14.

15.

16.

17.

18.

19.

My Creative Climate

What do you need to be at your creative best? List the elements found in your creative environment. For instance, what time of the day is most conducive to your ability to be creative?

1.

2.

3.

4.

5.

6.

A Spectrum of Creativity Techniques

C R E A T I V I T Y

Compare and combine

Risk taking

Expand and shrink

Ask "what's good?" and "what if?"

Transform your viewpoint

In another sequence

Visit other places

Incubate

Trigger concepts

Youth's advantage

Risky Business

I commit to the following risk: _____

_____

_____

_____
                              Signature

_____
Witness Signature

"Behold the turtle.
He makes progress only when
he sticks his neck out."

—James Conan Bryant

Your Creative Spectrum: Compare and Combine

Compare

To compare, take concepts and explore them by using analogies, similies, metaphors, or figures of speech that make a comparison between objects or ideas by using the word "like." (e.g. "The computer is like a human's brain.")

1. **Complete these comparisons:**

   Memo writing is like _____ because _____

   Hiring an exmployee is like _____ because _____

   Completing this task is like _____ because _____

   Memo writing and _____ are different in these ways:

   _____

2. **Now, think of a problem facing you. Create an analogy.**

   _____

   because _____

3. **List three ways your problem is like your analogy:**

   Because _____

   Because _____

   Because _____

4. **Now, how can these help solve your problem?**

Combine

To combine, take a problem or idea and combine it with something else and play with the possibilities. For example, if you combine floor and perfume, you might think of scented carpets, foot perfume, or vacuum cleaners that spread scents. Identify a project you have not completed. Combine it with one of the following words and identify ten combinations.

destiny	sunshine	game	wood
beverage	travel	nutrition	computer
book	leisure	aging	construction

10.	5.
9.	4.
8.	3.
7.	2.
6.	1.

Your Creative Spectrum: Risk Taking

Risk-taking is a vital part of creativity. Without it, the best one can hope for is good—maybe great. But superior demands that the idea be different, and different is a risk. Healthy risks are calculated risks. Determine the pros and cons of the risk venture. This method could be as simple as listing all of the positives and negatives about taking the risk or not taking the risk. The bottom line is that you must decide if the gain will be greater than any possible pain.

How can you become a successful risk taker?

- Assess your risk-taking quotient; challenge your assumptions.
- Accept that you will be criticized for taking risks.
- Establish a firm goal before initiating risk.
- Minimize risk by managing information, your control, and time.
- Be sure all the pieces are in place before you launch an idea—but don't wait for perfection.
- Size up the resistance; where, from whom, how strong.
- Break the risk down into smaller steps or over several time periods.
- Share the risk. That means sharing your vision, too.
- Keep everyone informed; your team, your boss. . . .
- Learn to be flexible, to roll with the punches.
- Learn from what you did. Always go back and evaluate what happened, the decision, the process.
- Stretch yourself; practice taking risks in all areas of your life.
- Reward yourself for taking a risk.

Questions to ask

1. How do you evaluate the risks you take?
2. How does your boss evaluate the risks you take?
3. Have you ever had ideas that didn't succeed or that someone else got credit for because you didn't risk?
4. What do you have "in the works" that is risky?
5. What do you want to do about your level of risk-taking?

> "Many great ideas have been lost because the people who had them couldn't stand being laughed at."
>
> —Fritz Peris

Your Creative Spectrum:
Expand and Shrink

This is a process of blowing an idea (conceptual level) or object (physical level) out of proportion—or shrinking it down to a smaller scale. For instance, you could expand the idea of window curtains to wall curtains. You could shrink the object of window curtains to camera shutters. Take the process of delegation and expand and shrink it on the conceptual and/or physical level:

Expand   **Shrink**

Now, think of your most recent issue, problem, or idea—and expand and shink it.

Expand   **Shrink**

Your Creative Spectrum:
Ask What's Good? and What If?

Ask "what's good?"

This question is especially helpful when faced with a disaster, when something terrible has happened to you: your home was burglarized, you lost your wallet with $1000 cash, you just messed up your big project. Asking what's good about it will give you a new perspective, new ideas for next steps and a new lease on life.

You've just lost your job. What's good about it?

Ask "what if?"

This question is useful when faced with ideas that are considered sacred truisms such as, "if it's not broken, don't fix it." When someone says it can't be done, ask yourself, "what if?" This is a process for exploring alternatives. Often corporate truisms of the past inhibit creativity and growth for the future.

Identify a sacred truism. Then ask, "what if?"

Your Creative Spectrum: Transform Your Viewpoint

This technique causes you to see the problem in different ways. Often a different perspective gives you new solutions. You can examine a problem through someone else's eyes, during a different era, from a different perspective or under different circumstances.

The U.S. Department of Labor predicts that by the year 2000, 85% of new entrants to the work force will be women and minorities and 14% will be white males. How might each of these view the situation?

☐ **Women**	☐ **Black male college senior**
☐ **Foreigners**	☐ **18-year-old white male**
☐ **Your spouse**	☐ **Female high school graduate**
☐ **Your CEO**	☐ **Abraham Lincoln**

Think of your current project

Think of the biggest project on your desk right now. Identify different ways it could be viewed and what those views might be.

Time	Different Circumstances
Last year	Money no object
1950	You are CEO
2010	Company moves to Hawaii

Change your perspective

If you are positive about the project, look at it negatively. If you are negative, look at it positively.

> "...it's amazing what you can do when you put your mind to it."
>
> —Buckminster Fuller

Your Creative Spectrum: In Another Sequence

This technique suggests that you explore other sequences. What if you did the steps in the process in a different order? What if you did the process backward? What if you looked at the problem backward? What if the problem was actually the solution? In the insurance industry, what if you got death benefits before you died? Prudential came up with the living benefit life insurance. It pays people who are suffering terminal illness their death benefits before they die.

1. **Think about your evening family routine.**

   What if you did it backward for a week? What are the advantages? Disadvantages?

2. **Think of a problem you have right now.**

   What if that problem was the solution?

3. **Think about the information flow in your department.**

   Draw a simple flowchart. What if the flow of information were reversed? Maybe it shouldn't be reversed, but is there a more logical, efficient flow?

Your Creative Spectrum: Visit Other Places

When trying to find creative solutions, it is important to look in both usual and unusual places. This demands that you leave your world of business and find ideas in other worlds. One innovation that resulted from using this technique is the ability to make cookware that can go from the freezer to the oven. Manufacturing took the concept from space technology. Use other fields to broaden your creative search. Typically, the flow of information in our society follows a specific order:

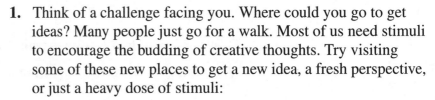

- Military.

- Medicine.

- Business.

- Toys.

- Education.

1. Think of a challenge facing you. Where could you go to get ideas? Many people just go for a walk. Most of us need stimuli to encourage the budding of creative thoughts. Try visiting some of these new places to get a new idea, a fresh perspective, or just a heavy dose of stimuli:

   Toy store, hike in the mountains, ocean, walk along the lake shore, zoo, woods, meadow, farm, book store, large magazine store, car ride in the country, lying in your backyard on a starry night, lunch with a friend, long soak in the bathtub, art gallery, museum, movie, New York, library, factory, candy store, housewares store, hardware store, sunset, sunrise, park, or any other personally stimulating place.

2. Identify a challenge facing you in the next six months. Where could you go to get ideas? Be specific. In addition, don't be limited by physical places. For example, you could "go to" a magazine, a video, or a book.

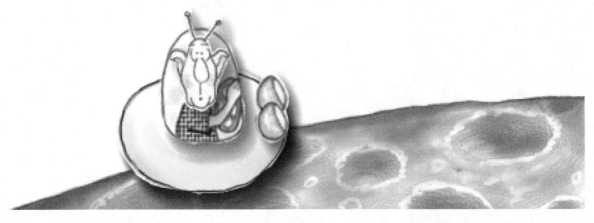

Your Creative Spectrum: Incubate

Remember when you were in school and your English teacher tried to encourage you to write your report early so that you could "put it on the back burner?" She was actually helping you tap into your subconscious, where your creative sparks really fly!

The incubate technique simply means that after you have gathered and reviewed data and information, you let all of it sit and gurgle in your brain. It needs to simmer on the back burner to get your creative juices flowing. This is the time to do something else, something unrelated to your idea. Or, try sleeping or dreaming on it.

Dream on!

Have you ever awakened in the middle of the night with the perfect solution to a problem? You knew it was too good to forget, but by morning you did forget it! How can you make your dreams work for you?

1. Before you go to sleep, think about the problem. Think about it like a metaphor. The subconscious likes metaphors.

2. Just before falling asleep, give yourself a mental suggestion that you will remember what you dream.

3. When you awake, don't open your eyes, since the stimuli will immediately wipe out the memory of your dream. Instead, review the dream.

4. Open your eyes and immediately write it down. It helps to keep a pen and paper (or tape recorder) by your bed with light available. (There are some lighted note pads and pens made just for this purpose.)

5. In the morning, review your dreams, looking for patterns and re-occurrences.

Incubate (cont.)

Why does this work? Your conscious mind can focus on only one idea at a time. Your subconscious, however, can focus on several at once. It allows your mind to wander and connect ideas that are floating around.

Looking for creative ideas? Perhaps the best you can do is to "give it a break!"

*   Think of a challenge that's been facing you. How can you "give it a break?"

*   Where can you go to get your mind off of it?

*   Does dreaming of a solution seem feasible? How and when will you do this?

*   What prevents you from using this technique more often? How can you change that?

Sometimes setting a date with yourself and putting it on the calendar helps. Tell yourself something like, "Self, I will think about this and make a decision on October 30." Then, do it! Next time, you'll believe yourself, and it will work better.

Your Creative Spectrum: Trigger Concepts

This technique can be personalized easily. You may choose to create your own list of favorite words, using prepositions or nouns. Some people build a creativity file of stimulating articles and pictures. Still others pose their situation as a question and then open a favorite book, dictionary, or newspaper and blindly point to a passage to start an idea from the connection. Still others use items in the room.

1. Choose two items in this room. Now, decide how those items would enhance a bathtub.

2. Think of a concern you have. Find a newspaper or book. Point to a passage in it without looking. How did those words provide insight to your concern?

3. Think of something you must change. Use the following list of trigger words to identify how you might change it.

   - Combine.

   - Delegate.

   - Increase.

   - Magnify.

   - Rearrange.

   - Personalize.

   - Simplify.

   - Computerize.

   - Subtract.

   - Quicken.

   - Reduce.

   - Cut Cost.

Your Creative Spectrum: Youth's Advantage

This is the technique of seeing things as a child does. Use these guidelines to be:

Innocent	To the child everything is fresh and new.
Miniature	Everything else is larger than the child.
Curious	Children want to explore everything.
Literal	"Take a hike" means to go on a hike.
Honest	Do not filter; "out of the mouths of babes."
Fun-seeking	Look for the fun; children always do.
Positive	Children are Pollyannas.

1. Your area has been chosen to pilot a new computer system. See this challenge from a youth's advantage.

    Innocent   _____

    Miniature   _____

    Curious   _____

    Literal   _____

    Honest   _____

    Fun-seeking   _____

    Positive   _____

2. Think of a "people" problem you are having. How would a child handle it? What might that child say?

The Company's Creative Past

"Heavier than air flying machines are impossible."

—Lord Kelvin
President, Royal Society, Co. 1895

Creativity Climate Survey

Directions   Measure the creativity climate that you are working in today. Respond using the following scale.

Answer key   1 = Strongly Agree, 2 = Agree, 3 = Uncertain, 4 = Disagree, 5 = Strongly Disagree

		Agree				Disagree
1.	My work is criticized without letting me explain.	1	2	3	4	5
2.	I am encouraged to be as creative as possible.	1	2	3	4	5
3.	Management judges employees' actions.	1	2	3	4	5
4.	Management allows flexibility on the job.	1	2	3	4	5
5.	New ideas are not valued in this job.	1	2	3	4	5
6.	Management is open to new ideas and change.	1	2	3	4	5
7.	My manager controls how or when I do my work.	1	2	3	4	5
8.	My manager understands the problems that I handle in my job.	1	2	3	4	5
9.	Management shows little respect or interest in new ideas.	1	2	3	4	5
10.	My manager respects my feelings, values and ideas.	1	2	3	4	5
11.	Little flexibility exists in the work environment.	1	2	3	4	5
12.	My manager protects my creative ideas.	1	2	3	4	5
13.	My ideas have been presented as someone else's ideas.	1	2	3	4	5
14.	I am respected for the diversity I bring.	1	2	3	4	5
15.	I have to be careful in talking with management so I will be understood.	1	2	3	4	5
16.	Management interacts with employees without projecting higher status or power.	1	2	3	4	5
17.	Management takes credit for employees' ideas.	1	2	3	4	5
18.	My manager respects and trusts me.	1	2	3	4	5
19.	Management is not open with information.	1	2	3	4	5
20.	I am provided opportunities to learn and experience new things.	1	2	3	4	5
21.	Management treats everyone the same.	1	2	3	4	5

		Agree				Disagree
22.	The organization's climate stimulates creativity.	1	2	3	4	5
23.	My manager rarely gives moral support to employees.	1	2	3	4	5
24.	I can express my ideas openly and honestly to my manager.	1	2	3	4	5
25.	Sometimes I feel powerless and inadequate.	1	2	3	4	5
26.	My manager communicates ideas so that they can be understood but does not insist that I agree.	1	2	3	4	5
27.	My manager makes it clear who is the boss.	1	2	3	4	5
28.	I have time and resources to be creative.	1	2	3	4	5
29.	Management checks everything to ensure that work is done right.	1	2	3	4	5
30.	I am rewarded for taking appropriate risks.	1	2	3	4	5
31.	Management cannot admit to mistakes.	1	2	3	4	5
32.	Management describes situations clearly and objectively.	1	2	3	4	5
33.	My manager is dogmatic; I can't change my manager's mind.	1	2	3	4	5
34.	My manager provides appropriate direction and feedback.	1	2	3	4	5
35.	Management thinks that their ideas are always correct.	1	2	3	4	5
36.	I am encouraged to have direct customer contact.	1	2	3	4	5

"The future belongs to those societies that. . . enable the characteristically human elements of our nature to flourish, to those societies that encourage diversity rather than conformity."

—Carl Sagan

SCORING   **Creativity Climate Survey Scoring**

Put the numbers that you assigned to each statement in the appropriate blanks. Add them to subtotal each climate descriptor. Add together the subtotals in each column to obtain the final scores.

1. _____   2. _____
3. _____   4. _____
5. _____ **C**ritical   6. _____ **O**pen-minded
   subtotal _____   subtotal _____

7. _____   8. _____
9. _____   10. _____
11. _____ **L**ashing 12. _____ **P**erceptive
   subtotal _____   subtotal _____

13. _____   14. _____
15. _____   16. _____
17. _____ **O**pportunistic 18. _____ **E**qual
   subtotal _____   subtotal _____

19. _____   20. _____
21. _____   22. _____
23. _____ **S**olo   24. _____ **N**urturing
   subtotal _____   subtotal _____

25. _____   26. _____
27. _____   28. _____
29. _____ **E**gotistical 30. _____ **E**ncouraging
   subtotal _____   subtotal _____

31. _____   32. _____
33. _____   34. _____
35. _____ **D**ogmatic 36. _____ **D**escriptive
   subtotal _____   subtotal _____

Closed Score _____   **Opened Score** _____

Total Score Guide

No matter what your climate score or label is, you are now aware of your climate's tone. This can provide the information and foundation to foster improving your creativity climate.

Closed		Opened	
18–41	Closed	18–41	Opened
42–65	Neutral	42–65	Neutral
66–90	Opened	66–90	Closed

Opened Climates

Open-minded

Encourage flexibility and creativity.

1. Allow employees to schedule their own work and deadlines as much as possible.

2. Allow employees to experiment with using creative approaches and techniques.

3. See employees as creative people by recognizing creative efforts.

4. Encourage total group involvement in creative efforts by establishing work teams.

5. Budget for creative efforts.

Perceptive

See things from your employees' viewpoints.

1. Ensure that the work is rewarding both in a professional and personal way (e.g. interesting and significant).

2. Encourage a participative atmosphere by asking for and acting upon employees' input.

3. Protect creative employees' from dullards who don't understand what makes them tick.

4. Be a creative role model.

5. Minimize the risk factors and share the responsibility (e.g. giving research time).

Equal

Respect everyone for the diversity each brings.

1. Give employees credit by implementing ideas without editing or changing them.

2. Enter employees' work in competition.

3. Ensure that ideas are implemented well.

4. Individualize leadership techniques and styles that fit the needs of each employee.

Nurturing

Stimulate free expression of ideas.

1. Listen to creative ideas with interest.

2. Provide creative pollen through speakers and other learning opportunities.

3. Foster creativity in group work as well as in individual projects.

4. Provide the necessary climate stimulus (e.g., a creative room, purple office, quiet space or whatever it takes).

5. Accommodate regeneration needs through paid time off, sabbaticals, etc.

Encouraging

Encourage employees to find answers creatively.

1. Provide the time needed to do so by delaying other work or delegating to another person.

2. Open up resources and avenues for exploration.

3. Serve as a catalyst with actions (not just words) to employees' creative endeavors (e.g., get them what they need).

4. Positively reinforce and reward risks.

5. Allow freedom and opportunity for self-expression.

6. Identify those who exhibit creativity and select them as mentors.

Descriptive

Give clear objectives and specific feedback.

1. State the purpose of the task in specific—not vague—terms.

2. Balance structure with opportunity for creative expression.

3. Provide input through direct customer contact.

4. Give explicit, as well as supportive, feedback.

Killer Phrases

Killer phrases, coined by Dr. Sidney J. Parnes, can stop creativity in its tracks—bring it to a dead end halt. If our company is to foster a creative climate, the first thing we need to do is identify our common killer phrases—those that prevent creativity.

List as many killer phrases as you can think of:

The second thing we need to do is eliminate these killer phrases.

Where Can Creativity Flourish?

Open-minded

Perceptive

Equal

Nurturing

Encouraging

Descriptive

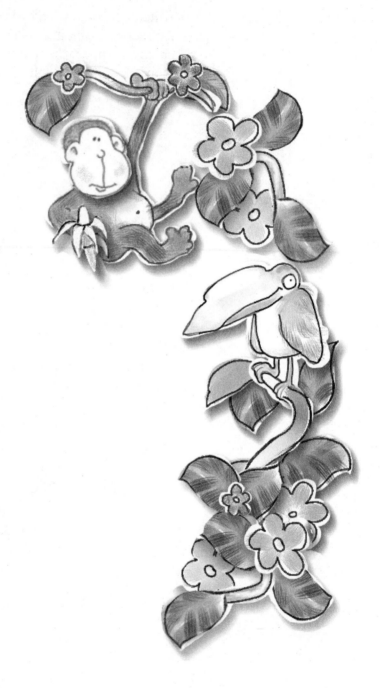

Brainstorming

Brainstorming is based on a belief that quantity breeds quality. The more ideas generated, the greater the chance that one will prove to be a high quality solution. The key to successful brainstorming is to suspend judgment. All ideas are good. The nine basic rules used to guide a brainstorming session are:

1. Suspend judgment. Failure to follow this rule is the major reason why some brainstorming sessions do not produce the expected results.

2. Freewheeling is encouraged. All ideas that come to mind are valued. The wilder the ideas, the better.

3. Quantity is wanted. The goal is to have many ideas.

4. "Piggybacking" is welcome. Participants are encouraged to build on each other's ideas or generate a number of ideas using a previous one as a stimulus.

5. Post all ideas as you go.

6. A member may ask for clarification of a suggestion. However, it is important to avoid any questions that are directed to "how" and "why."

7. Allow enough time.

8. Encourage humor and playfulness.

9. Assign both a facilitator and a recorder.

Brainstorming (cont.)

When conducting a brainstorming session, always remind participants of the goals of brainstorming and of the nine rules of brainstorming. It will be the job of the facilitator to see to it that the rules are enforced.

Variations

1. It is sometimes helpful to send out a statement of the problem to team members a few days before your meeting time and request that they bring ideas with them.

2. Be prepared to offer "stimulators" to the team if they become stuck, or persist in looking at the problem from only one direction.

3. Push to generate "X" more ideas.

4. Push to generate as many ideas as possible in "X" minutes.

5. Structured brainstorming follows the same rules. The only difference is that before the entire team begins to brainstorm ideas, participants write ideas on paper or index cards. The ideas are collected and redistributed. It doesn't matter if participants get their own ideas. The purpose is to add anonymity to the process so participants can bring up ideas with which they may otherwise be uncomfortable. The written ideas are listed in a round robin fashion. When all ideas are out, large team brainstorming begins.

6. *Add an Idea* is an activity conducted in silence. Each individual gets a stack of cards. After you write your idea, you will pass the card to your left. You will get a card from your right, read it, write another idea and then pass two cards to your left. You will now get two cards, read them both, write a third card and pass all three. This will continue until one entire circuit has been completed (ten people means ten rounds).

    There is one difference from brainstorming. Rounds get slower because people need more time to read the ideas and answer the questions. The facilitator collects the cards and categorizes them. This may be done immediately following the brainstorming or at a later time.

7. Sometimes individuals write their ideas on Post-it Notes. This allows for easier categorizing.

What Can You Do?

Brainstorm as many ideas as you can that will enhance your personal creative ability.

Lighting Others' Creativity

As you have discovered in this program, the creative process is impacted by two environments—the environment within each person and the environment in which the person is creating. You have an opportunity to light others' creativity. It begins with your attitude toward others' creative efforts. Your choices are to be either CLOSED or OPENED to their creative endeavors. Consider the significance of the following quotations:

> "The best executive is the one who has the sense enough to pick good men to do what he wants done, and self-restraint enough to keep from meddling with them while they do it."
>
> —Theodore Roosevelt

My thoughts:

_____

_____

_____

_____

_____

_____

_____

_____

_____

_____

_____

Lighting Others' Creativity (cont.)

> "There are two ways of spreading light. . . by the candle, or the mirror that reflects it."
>
> —Edith Wharton

My thoughts:

_____

_____

_____

_____

Who can I encourage to be more creative?

_____

_____

_____

_____

How can I do this?

_____

_____

_____

_____

What should I discuss with them?

_____

_____

_____

_____

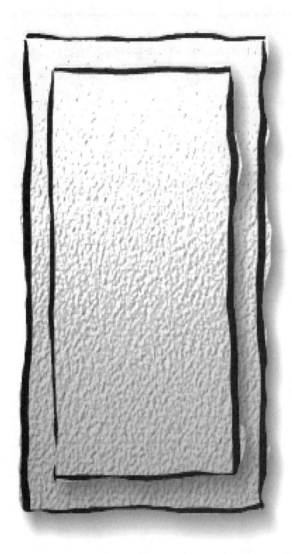

Creatively Yours

Date: _____

To be more creative in the future, I will:

1. _____

2. _____

3. _____

To help others be more creative, I will:

1. _____

2. _____

3. _____

To help ensure my company has the most creative climate available, I will:

1. _____

2. _____

3. _____

Creatively Yours,

_____
Signature

widen your spectrum

Reading List

Adams, James L. *The Care and Feeding of Ideas: A Guide to Encouraging Creativity.* Massachusetts: Addison Wesley Publishing Company, Inc. 1986.

Barker, Joel. *Future Edge.* New York: William Morrow and Company, Inc. 1992.

de Bono, Edward. *Six Thinking Hats.* New York: Little, Brown Publishers. 1992.

Drucker, Peter F. *Innovation and Entrepeneurship.* New York: Harper & Row Publishers. 1985.

Gross, T. Scott. *Positively Outrageous Service.* New York: Mastermedia Limited. 1991.

Handy, Charles. *The Age of Unreason.* Massachusetts: Harvard Business School Press. 1990.

Hanks, Kurt, and Jay Parry. *Wake Up Your Creative Genius.* California: William Kaufmann, Inc. 1994.

Higgins, James M. *101 Creative Problem Solving Techniques.* Florida: The New Management Publishing Company. 1994.

Mattimore, Bryan W. *99% Inspiration.* New York: AMACOM. 1993.

Michalko, Michael. *Thinkertoys.* California: Ten Speed Press. 1991.

Ray, Michael, and Rochelle Myers. *Creativity in Business.* New York: Doubleday & Company, Inc. 1986.

Noble, Sara, ed. *301 Great Management Ideas from America's Most Innovative Small Companies.* Massachusetts: Inc. Publishing. 1991.

von Oech, Roger. *A Kick in the Seat of the Pants.* New York: Harper & Row Publisher. 1986

von Oech, Roger. *A Whack on the Side of the Head.* New York: Harper & Row Publisher. 1983.

> "Life is either a daring adventure, or nothing."
>
> —Helen Keller

Session Evaluation

1. **Share your impression of the presenter:**

2. **Give your evaluation of the materials:**

3. **List any topics you'd like to see added or subtracted from the content:**

4. **My experiences in *Widen Your Spectrum* were:**

My Creative Viewpoint

Share your thoughts about creativity by completing the following:

Q. The most recent creative action I took was to

_____

_____

_____

13. What I enjoy most about being creative is

_____

_____

_____

#. What I enjoy least about being creative is

_____

_____

_____

❊. When I am being creative I feel

_____

_____

_____

▼. Three things that I fear about being creative are

_____

_____

_____

"Imagination is the beginning of creation. We imagine what we desire; we will what we imagine; and at last we create what we will."
—George Bernard Shaw

A Taste of Creativity: Definition

How does creativity taste?

How does creativity look? Draw a picture of it.

Define creativity:

> "Discovery consists of looking at the same thing as everyone else and thinking something different."
>
> —Albert Szent-Györgyi

So You Think You Have an Idea. . .

My idea is:

_____

_____

What excites me about it is:

_____

_____

I will benefit from this idea by:

_____

_____

Others will benefit from this idea by:

_____

_____

My vision for completing this idea is:

_____

_____

The most difficult part, or greatest hurdle, is:

_____

_____

The resources I will use to succeed are:

    My resources_____

    Others' resources_____

I'm going to be wildly successful, and this will:

    Look like _____

    Feel like _____

    Sound like _____

    Taste like _____

From Here to. . .

My next five steps are these, which will require the identified resources and will be completed by the date I listed:

	Resources	Date
1.		
2.		
3.		
4.		
5.		

I'd like my "Idea Coach" to help me by:

Contingency plan   **If I run into problems I can:**

a) **Give up.**

b) **Blame my boss.**

c) **Eat two Hershey bars and a bag of potato chips.**

d) **Beat myself up.**

e) **Call my Idea Coach at:**

. . . There

What's Next?

Do it! Do it! Do it! Do it! Do it! Do it! Do it! Do it! Do it! Do it! Do it! Do it!

Do it! Do it! Do it! Do it! Do it! Do it! Do it! Do it! Do it! Do it! Do it! Do it!

Do it! Do it! Do it! Do it! Do it! Do it! Do it! Do it! Do it! Do it! Do it! Do it!

Do it! Do it! Do it! Do it! Do it! Do it! Do it! Do it! Do it! Do it! Do it! Do it!

Do it! Do it! Do it! Do it! Do it! Do it! Do it! Do it! Do it! Do it! Do it! Do it!

Do it! Do it! Do it! Do it! Do it! Do it! Do it! Do it! Do it! Do it! Do it! Do it!

Do it! Do it! Do it! Do it! Do it! Do it! Do it! Do it! Do it! Do it! Do it! Do it!

Do it! Do it! Do it! Do it! Do it! Do it! Do it! Do it! Do it! Do it! Do it! Do it!

Do it! Do it! Do it! Do it! Do it! Do it! Do it! Do it! Do it! Do it! Do it! Do it!

Do it! Do it! Do it! Do it! Do it! Do it! Do it! Do it! Do it! Do it! Do it! Do it!

Do it! Do it! Do it! Do it! Do it! Do it! Do it! Do it! Do it! Do it! Do it! Do it!

Do it! Do it! Do it! Do it! Do it! Do it! Do it! Do it! Do it! Do it! Do it! Do it!

Do it! Do it! Do it! Do it! Do it! Do it! Do it! Do it! Do it! Do it! Do it! Do it!

Do it! Do it! Do it! Do it! Do it! Do it! Do it! Do it! Do it! Do it! Do it! Do it!

Do it! Do it! Do it! Do it! Do it! Do it! Do it! Do it! Do it! Do it! Do it! Do it!

Do it! Do it! Do it! Do it! Do it! Do it! Do it! Do it! Do it! Do it! Do it! Do it!

Do it! Do it! Do it! Do it! Do it! Do it! Do it! Do it! Do it! Do it! Do it! Do it!

Do it! Do it! Do it! Do it! Do it! Do it! Do it! Do it! Do it! Do it! Do it! Do it!

Do it! Do it! Do it! Do it! Do it! Do it! Do it! Do it! Do it! Do it! Do it! Do it!

Do it! Do it! Do it! Do it! Do it! Do it! Do it! Do it! Do it! Do it! Do it! Do it!

Do it! Do it! Do it! Do it! Do it! Do it! Do it! Do it! Do it! Do it! Do it! Do it!

Do it! Do it! Do it! Do it! Do it! Do it! Do it! Do it! Do it! Do it! Do it! Do it!

Do it! Do it! Do it! Do it! Do it! Do it! Do it! Do it! Do it! Do it! Do it! Do it!

Do it! Do it! Do it! Do it! Do it! Do it! Do it! Do it! Do it! Do it! Do it! Do it!

Do it! Do it! Do it! Do it! Do it! Do it! Do it! Do it! Do it! Do it! Do it! Do it!

Do it! Do it! Do it! Do it! Do it! Do it! Do it! Do it! Do it! Do it! Do it! Do it!

Do it! Do it! Do it! Do it! Do it! Do it! Do it! Do it! Do it! Do it! Do it! Do it!

Do it! Do it! Do it! Do it! Do it! Do it! Do it! Do it! Do it! Do it! Do it! Do it!

Do it! Do it! Do it! Do it! Do it! Do it! Do it! Do it! Do it! Do it! Do it! Do it!

Getting Unstuck

Do things differently
- Visit a museum.
- Take a different route to work.
- Read a book you know you'll hate.
- Visit a building you've never been in.
- Make a phone call to a friend you've not talked to in over a year.
- Visit a kindergarten.
- Go for a swim.
- Go for a run.
- Listen to a different radio station.
- Walk around your block backward.
- Cross your eyes.
- Visit an art gallery.
- Take a shower.
- Watch a silent movie.
- Rent a 1950s video.
- Go dancing.

Visioning
- Think about your favorite sport.
- See the task completed.
- See the same situation in 1850; in 2010.
- Imagine yourself dancing with Fred Astaire or Ginger Rogers.
- See yourself in a blizzard.
- Envision yourself on a tropical island.
- Imagine you are a millionaire.

Word ideas
- Play Scrabble.
- Read the dictionary.
- Read the sports page—or not.
- Do a cryptogram.
- Read a comic book.
- Visit a magazine stand, buy and read three you've never read.
- Look through the yellow pages.

Getting Unstuck (cont.)

Get ideas from others

- Hold a crazy idea meeting at lunch.
- Offer to pay $10 for every idea you use.
- Ask your child or someone under ten years young.
- Ask your father-in-law.
- Ask your child's teacher.
- Ask the librarian.
- Ask a cab driver.
- Start talking with someone, anyone, and ask them to challenge you and push you to continue.

Get crazy

- Wear a costume to work.
- Have a party.
- Read only the ads in a magazine.
- Watch TV with the sound off.
- Hire someone to figure it out.
- Blindly choose a word from the dictionary and list 25 ways it's related to your need.
- Play a computer game.
- Visit an arcade.
- Read children's books.

Time related

- Establish a completion time.
- Break the task into small parts; assign a reward to the completion of each.
- Establish a portion that must be done by a certain time. If successful, you quit; if not, work another hour.
- Poke a hole in the project. Do something, anything, for 15 minutes—then quit.

Stimulate your senses

- Eat an unusual fruit.
- Eat chocolate.
- Use an air scenting machine.
- Burn a scented candle.
- Go to sleep.
- Dream about it.
- Listen to music you don't usually listen to.
- Listen to your favorite music.
- Listen to an environmental tape of the ocean; jungle.

Getting Unstuck (cont.)

Writing related

- Use a mind map on a large piece of paper.
- Start writing with crayons.
- Write with scented markers.
- Start writing and don't stop for 20 minutes, no matter what is flowing from the pen.
- Write about all the things you can't do.
- Write the plan from your secretary's viewpoint.
- Write with colored chalk on your sidewalk.
- Write as fast as you can.

Shock your dominance

- Cross your arms the opposite way for five minutes.
- Cross your legs the opposite way for five minutes.
- Use your more dominant eye to read a magazine article.
- List ideas with your non-dominant hand.
- Doodle with your non-dominant hand.
- Call someone and keep the receiver on the ear opposite the one you usually use.
- Breathe through only one nostril at a time for ten minutes.

Your favorites

_____

_____

_____

_____

_____

_____

_____

_____

_____

_____

_____

For other organizational ideas, read "Bright Ideas" by Michael Michalko in _Training & Development Magazine,_ 1994.

The Five R's of Creativity

Number in order the steps in the creative process. Then, connect the numbers in sequence.

___ **Review the data**

___ **Refine**
(connect to #1)

Recognize the spark ___

___ **Rest the data**

___ **Realize the need**

> "Ruth made a big mistake when he gave up pitching."
>
> —Tris Speaker, 1921

Steps in the Creative Process

1. **Realize the need.**

   Realize the need by stating a specific idea or objective:

   _____

   _____

   _____

   _____

2. **Review the data.**

   Review the data using all of your research skills and sources. Where can you locate the information for the goal you set? Stretch yourself. Go beyond the typical sources.

   _____

   _____

   _____

   _____

3. **Rest the data.**

   The key term here is rest or incubate or ferment. Let all the information you've collected sit and gurgle in your brain. You need to put it on the "back burner" to simmer and let your creative juices work. Go do something else, something unrelated to your idea. Or, try sleeping or dreaming on it. Remember:

   - Let the idea ferment.

   - Come back to it later and "see" it differently.

   - Time may provide more data.

   - Try dreaming on it.

   _____

   _____

   _____

   _____

Steps in the Creative Process (cont.)

4. **Recognize the spark.**

   Creativity comes in flashes and sparks. Be prepared to recognize it and to capture it in writing.

   - Carry pencil and paper with you—or have it available everywhere you go.

   - If you awaken in the middle of the night, write down those ideas your dreams just gave you.

   Now, list five additional ways you can ensure that you'll capture those creative ideas:

   _____

   _____

   _____

   _____

   _____

5. **Refine.**

   Take your newly formed creative flash and refine it. Decide what works and what doesn't. You'll act as judge to determine your idea's fate.

   J **ustify it's existence** (positives).

   U **ndermine its development** (negatives).

   D **elay your personal biases and attitudes** (be neutral).

   G **enerate the decision** (use a process).

   E **xecute your decision** (action).

   JUDGE this idea:

   Winning is everything.

Eyedeas

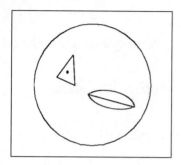

1. _____
2. _____
3. _____

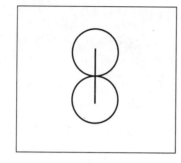

1. _____
2. _____
3. _____

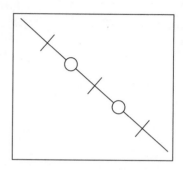

1. _____
2. _____
3. _____

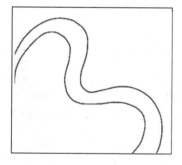

1. _____
2. _____
3. _____

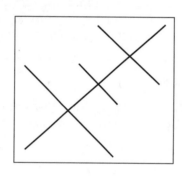

1. _____
2. _____
3. _____

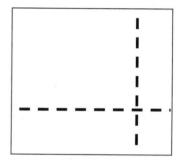

1. _____
2. _____
3. _____

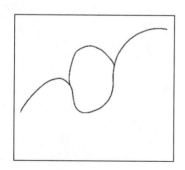

1. _____
2. _____
3. _____

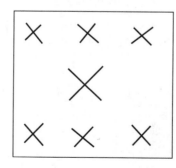

1. _____
2. _____
3. _____

1. _____
2. _____
3. _____

Your Creative Style

Attributes:

Advantages:

Problems:

Kid's Game

List at least ten ways you can use the elements and rules of the game of Monopoly to facilitate your next staff meeting.

1. _____

2. _____

3. _____

4. _____

5. _____

6. _____

7. _____

8. _____

9. _____

10. _____

11. _____

12. _____

13. _____

14. _____

15. _____

Chapter Seven:

Learning Activities

This book provides a variety of experiential learning activities and energizers that you may use in your workshops.

WHAT'S IN THIS CHAPTER

This chapter is divided into two segments:

- **Workshop Activities**

  Activities found in the one-day, half-day and one-hour training workshops. These activities are similar to those found in the workshops. They have simply been rewritten to be readily plugged into other workshops. They are presented as self-contained, independent activities.

- **Optional Activities**

  Optional activities not found in the workshops.

Each activity is presented in an easy-to-read format that contains the following elements:

- **Objective**

  The reason you would choose the activity; what you would hope to accomplish by conducting the activity.

- **Time**

  An approximate amount of time the activity takes; actual time is often due to the number of participants and how talkative they are.

- **Materials**

  A list of supplies and handouts you will need to conduct the activity.

- **Procedure**

   A step-by-step narrative that tells you what you need to do.

- **Debrief**

   A questioning or summarizing process which you will use to bring the activity to a close.

How To Use These Activities

You can use these activities in many ways. You may use them specifically for teaching creativity skills, or as a part of other workshops. Creativity techniques are of course useful whether you are teaching selling skills, team building, stress management or diversity awareness.

Most of these activities have been designed for 12–20 participants. If the activities are to be completed in small groups, the procedure will say how many should be in these groups. Use your creativity to break the large group into small groups (e.g., color of their shirts, birthdays, singing songs, number of children, favorite color, part of country they came from, counting off backward.)

You will find these activities useful:

- To enhance workshops you now conduct.

- As a basis for a brief presentation, for example at an ASTD meeting.

- As they are written within the workshops.

- To build your own workshops.

- To stimulate your creativity to design your own activities.

And the optional activities, of course, could be substituted in the workshops in Chapters 3, 4 and 5.

Feel free to customize the activities to meet your specific needs.

Activities based on the workshops in this book begin on page 195. Optional activites begin on page 243.

Workshop Activities

TRAINER'S NOTES

Meet the Creative Me

Objective

To introduce participants to each other using a creative technique and to push participants into right-brain thinking.

Time

- 20 minutes.

Materials

- Handout *Meet the Creative Me* (p. 138).

Procedure

1. *ASK* each participant to complete the handout, *Meet the Creative Me*. Give them your answers to these questions as a model for them to follow and to ease any discomfort they may have in opening up their creative side to the group. Use the sample answers in the handout or create your own.

   My name is: _____ (Zesty) _____

   I am a(n): _____ (time traveler) _____

   Using the five senses, I would describe myself as:

   I look like: _____ (a whirlwind) _____

   I smell like: _____ (a sea breeze) _____

   I feel like: _____ (a bubble) _____

   I sound like: _____ (perking coffee) _____

   I taste like: _____ (a hot fudge sundae) _____

   My latest adventure was:

   _____ (reading a ghost story to Robert Redford _____

   _____ while eating macadamia nuts in a hot tub.) _____

2. *HAVE* participants introduce themselves to the large group by sharing their answers.

3. *ASK* if anyone felt uncomfortable using this format for introductions. Discuss the following points:

   - This was a right-brain way of introducing yourself.

   - Some people feel uncomfortable using the right brain to reveal "self." They feel naked, unprotected.

4. *DISCUSS* the following quotation by William James:

> "Human beings can alter their lives by altering their attitudes of mind."
>
> —William James

What are your thoughts about this quotation? Use the discussion to illustrate these points:

- People can change.

- Our attitudes affect the way we behave.

- If we think we are something, then we will be just that.

5. *ASK* the following question:

What's the worst thing that can happen to you during this program? Expect answers such as:

- I will be asked to do something I cannot do.

- I will look stupid or foolish.

- I will be asked to do something I do not believe in.

- I will not be creative.

Debrief

CLOSE with these remarks:

Creative people will be creative, no matter which job they perform. There is a company which has the following rule: "The only rule in this company is that there are no rules." In this program, there are no rules. Walk around when you like. Observe and try activities in the room at your leisure. Take breaks when you need them. Sit on the floor if you like.

Notes

- _____

- _____

- _____

- _____

- _____

- _____

- _____

<u>TRAINER'S NOTES</u>

Can Creativity Be Defined?

Objective

To allow participants to create a definition of creativity, to introduce the topic of creativity, to say there are no "right" answers, and to introduce the idea that we force ourselves into rules.

Time

- 20 minutes.

Materials

- Handout *Can Creativity Be Defined?* (p. 139).

- Overhead *Define Creativity* (p. 265).

- Overhead *Making of the New* (p. 266).

- Crayons.

Procedure

1. *ASK* participants to break into groups according to height. Do not give any other instructions. Many may get hung up on doing it right. Introduce the idea that in creativity there are "no rules." We impose our own rules. There are many ways to break into groups "according to height." (e.g., line up and split into X groups; tall, average and short into three groups; one tall, one average and one short in each group; or anyway because we all "have height.")

2. *REFER* to the handout *Can Creativity Be Defined?* (p. 139) and *INTRODUCE* the activity by saying:

   It is important to have a definition for creativity. We need to know it when we see it. In your groups, come up with a definition, a description and a symbol for creativity. Be prepared to share your ideas with the larger group and feel free to use the flip chart for your symbols.

3. When all groups have completed this activity, *ASK* representatives from the groups to share their ideas.

4. Use the overhead *Define Creativity* (p. 265) to record their responses.

5. *SHARE* the definition of creativity on the overhead *Making of the New* (p. 266).

> "Making of the new and the
> rearranging of the old."
>
> —Mike Vance
> Disney Corporation

Other definitions for you to use as a guide to the discussion are:

- The ability to bring about a new idea or invention.
- The ability to be original.
- Making the new by rearranging the old.

Debrief   *SUMMARIZE* with the quotation at the bottom of the page, by saying:

> "Everything that can be invented has been invented."
>
> —Charles H. Duell
> (Director of U.S. Patent Office, 1899)

Duell's quotation is humorous, but he meant it most seriously. Compare what he is saying to the following quotation from the Bible: "There is nothing new under the sun," Ecclesiastes 1:9.

Point out that although the biblical quotation is not the same as Duell's quotation, they both illustrate an important fact about creativity—it takes what is and makes it different to bring about a new idea or invention.

Notes

- _____
- _____
- _____
- _____
- _____
- _____
- _____
- _____
- _____
- _____
- _____
- _____
- _____

TRAINER'S NOTES

Objective

Time

Materials

Procedure

My Creative Viewpoint

To help participants identify what they think and feel about creativity.

- 20 minutes.

- *My Creative Viewpoint* (p. 179).

1. *INTRODUCE* the activity by stating that it's important to get in touch with how we think and feel about creativity. *REFER* to the handout *My Creative Viewpoint* (p. 179) and have the participants complete the handout.

2. Once all have completed this page, ask participants to form triads and share answers to the statements. Following are suggested questions for you to ask after sharing each of the statements in a large group discussion:

Q. **"The most recent creative action I took was to. . ."**

ASK:

How long ago did most of these actions occur?

Use the responses to this question to point out that creativity happens daily in our lives. We need to be able to recognize it.

13. **"What I enjoy most about being creative is. . ."**

ASK:

How do you define "enjoy" as it is used here?

From this discussion, begin to get a profile on the rewards for being creative. These will be different for all people. Some will be intrinsic such as, "feels good," "satisfaction," etc. For others it may be extrinsic rewards such as, "recognition," "money," etc. Point out that both types of rewards are important and necessary to the successful encouragement of creative endeavors.

#. **"What I enjoy the least about being creative is. . ."**

ASK:

Do you think it is as possible to demotivate creativity as it is to encourage it?

Point out that it is, perhaps, more frequently done than the rewarding of creative works. Remind them about the rules that govern businesses. Mention the goal-oriented, results-minded atmosphere.

✳. **"When I am being creative I feel. . ."**

SAY:

Creativity is a process with defined steps. Some of your experiences with creativity have given you positive feelings about the process. However, other experiences may have given you negative feelings about the creative process.

Do not share the final statement in large groups. Ask them to circle the one that they fear most.

▼. **"Three things that I fear about being creative are:"**

Debrief

SUMMARIZE with the quote at the bottom of the page by Buckminster Fuller, saying,

"What message does Buckminster Fuller give us in this quotation about our creative viewpoints?"

Make the point that Fuller would probably say that we need to recognize that we are all creative—that we learn to suppress our creativity as we age.

> "Everyone is born an inventor."
>
> —Buckminster Fuller
> 20th Century American Engineer

Notes

- _____
- _____
- _____
- _____
- _____
- _____
- _____
- _____
- _____
- _____

Do You Know. . . ?

Objective

To introduce some interesting facts about creativity and to stimulate discussion and questions about the topic of creativity.

Time

• 40 minutes.

Materials

• Handout *Do You Know. . . ?* (p. 140).

Procedure

SAY: Creativity is a fascinating topic. I'd like to share some interesting facts about creativity. Please use the page in front of you to take notes. In addition, let's stop and discuss these as you have questions.

Make a point of reading the statements in the order on the handout starting with number 11, saying, "Do you know. . ."

11. That 86% of success in business at any level is dependent upon human relations and creative skills? Only 14% can be attributed to traditional scholastic pursuits.

8. That creativity and IQ are unrelated? A high IQ does not mean that a person is highly creative. Psychologists have tried to link IQ and creativity, but they haven't succeeded. We need knowledge, and the creative person wants to know it all: ancient history, astral projection, flower arranging and hog farming. But knowledge can't make a person creative.

2. That the supply of scientific information grows over 15% each year, and that by the year 2000 this could jump to 30%? How can we retain all of this? Do we need to? Is creativity an answer?

5. That Coke was originally invented as a medicine? Only when it no longer was medically sound did it become "The Real Thing." In the late 1800's John Pemberton invented a chemical mixture guaranteed to: whiten teeth, cleanse the mouth, harden and beautify gums and relieve mental and physical exhaustion. The first year he sold six glasses per day. In the 1980's there were 250 million servings sold per day. That is expected to multiply tenfold by the end of the century as Coke moves into new markets and attempts to become "a breakfast drink."

4. That the Nike shoe sole design was patterned after a waffle? We can find creative ideas everywhere—if we know how to look. Even though Bill Bowerman ruined his wife's waffle iron, he found a great idea by using it as the mold for a new type of shoe sole and can now afford as many waffle irons as he cares to purchase. This is a good example of a creativity technique known as compare and combine. (How is a waffle iron like a tennis shoe?)

7. That most people use only 2-3% of their total brain power? So what's the other 97% for? We once believed that we used 10% of our brain, but it is now believed that the only human to ever approach 10% was Einstein. We have an enormous amount of ability that is waiting to be tapped and developed.

6. That people spend 33 1/3% of their lives sleeping? For the average person that's 210,240 hours. So, why not use it creatively with continuous and focused dreaming? Dreaming and its connection with creativity is a fascinating topic that you may wish to explore after this session.

3. That the purpose of the court jester in the Middle Ages was to allow the king to receive an honest and open view of the world. The court jester didn't concern himself with looking "stupid." His job was to take a risk. Why was this important? Perhaps every company should have a court jester.

1. That by the age of seven most children are using about 10% of their creative ability? Why has this occurred? Socialization is a primary reason we box in our creativity.

10. That creativity can be learned? Creativity training has been a part of corporate America for several decades. It works.

9. That by age 40, adults are about 3% as creative as they are at age seven? We've learned to box it in. We all have an enormous amount of ability that's waiting to be tapped.

 ASK them to break into groups of four to five people to respond to the following questions:

*   What I found most interesting about these statements was. . .

*   What I still have a question about is. . .

*   The way that I see creativity is. . .

 If no one has asked about the numbering of questions—ask them why? The point to make is that we're often afraid to ask questions. We don't want to seem "stupid." Remember, there are no rules.

Debrief   *SUMMARIZE* by saying there is a lot that we know about creativity, but there is even more that we don't know. One thing is certain. Creativity is a fascinating topic and the more we learn the more fascinating it becomes.

Notes

*   _____

*   _____

*   _____

<u>TRAINER'S NOTES</u>	**Add an Idea**
Objective	To introduce an idea generating technique that is an adaptation of brainstorming and to help participants recognize that there are hundreds of ways to break through creativity blocks.
Time	• 25–35 minutes.
Materials	• Index cards.

Procedure

1. ***INTRODUCE*** the activity by asking how many people have been in brainstorming sessions. *Add an Idea* is an adaptation of brainstorming. Provide the following instructions:

   a. You have a stack of index cards in front of you. You will write one idea per card.

   b. The activity will be conducted in silence.

   c. After you write your idea, you will pass it to your left. You will get a card from your right, read it, write another idea and then pass two cards to your left.

   d. You will now get two cards, read them both, write a third card and pass all three.

   e. This will continue until one entire round has been completed (ten people means ten passes).

2. There is one difference from brainstorming. You can see that the ideas must be kept moving around the table. Therefore, if you can't think of an idea, write a question and people may begin to answer it. Some people may choose to answer that question, but many may not. The idea is to just keep things moving.

   • The topic we are going to brainstorm using this technique is: What are all the methods you can use to spark creativity?

   • Are there any questions?

   • Remember, we are looking for ways to spark creativity when you are blocked.

 You will need to ensure that the activity continues to move quickly. If you run short of time because you have a large group or people are taking more time than usual, you may need to end it before one complete round.

3. Once the group has completed the idea generation, ask participants to look through the stack of cards they have in front of them and to share:

- The most creative.

- The most practical.

- The one you like the best.

- The one that everyone could do.

- The zaniest one.

- Collect the index cards for typing later.

Debrief

Debrief this activity by asking the participants to share some advantages of this technique. The ideas may include:

- Many ideas in a short amount of time.

- Easy to divide into categories.

- Provides anonymity for suggestions if necessary.

Options

You may have the participants arrange the cards in categories and have them typed that way. This technique works on most any topic for which you need to generate ideas.

Notes

- _____

- _____

- _____

- _____

- _____

- _____

- _____

- _____

- _____

- _____

- _____

- _____

- _____

- _____

<u>TRAINER'S NOTES</u>	**Getting Out of the Box**
Objective	To explore the potential boxes participants may be in that prevent the flow of creative ideas and to discuss and practice ways to get outside the box.
Time	• 60–90 minutes.
Materials	• Handout *Nine Uncreative Boxes* (p. 142).
	• Handouts *Unbox Your Creativity* A–E (pp. 143-147).
	• Overhead *Nine Uncreative Boxes* (p. 270).
	• Overhead *Unbox Your Creativity* (p. 272).
	• Crayons.
	• One dollar bill, quarter.

Procedure

1. To open the activity, *ASK*: Why aren't we more creative?

2. Encourage ideas from the group and add any of the following if you wish:

    • We have routines that guide us and provide structure to operate on a daily basis. If we got up in the morning and tried to brainstorm 50 ways to cook an egg—we'd never get to work. We need routines.

    • We have developed attitudes or "boxes" that trap our creativity. We create many of these for ourselves. We box ourselves in with these attitudes.

3. Display the dollar bill and quarter and ask one participant to balance the quarter on the edge of the dollar bill.

    Solution: Fold the dollar accordion style and lay the quarter on top. Praise creative solutions to this problem. Explain that folding the dollar is a creative solution that takes us outside our box.

4. *SAY:* your *Nine Uncreative Boxes* handout (p. 142) lists and illustrates the boxes we may have put ourselves in that prevent creativity. Let's review them one by one. Color any of these that you feel box in your creativity.

- **Time Trapped**

  The time trapped box is one that captures many people. The creative process does take time, just as any other method of attacking a problem or tackling a project. Yet, business cannot succeed without creativity.

- **Risky Business Zone**

  The risky business zone warns of the dangers of taking a risk. Those trapped within this box view creativity as resulting in weird, unsound ideas. They fear taking risks. For creative ideas to have innovative results, risk is necessary. The year Babe Ruth hit the most home runs, he also struck out the most often.

- **Perfectionist Problem**

  Some people are sitting inside of the perfectionist problem box. Here, the person is constantly striving for perfection. Therefore, new and novel ways of doing things are never tried since they could possibly result in less than perfection. Schools teach us that it is bad to make mistakes. By the time you have finished high school you will have taken an average of 3952 quizzes, tests and exams. Getting the "right" answer is deeply ingrained in all of us. When asked if he wasn't dismayed about having failed at making a light bulb more than 1800 times, Thomas Edison said he wasn't bothered at all. He now knew 1800 ways NOT to make a light bulb!

- **Wright or Wrong Thinking**

  Wright or wrong thinking keeps many in the dark. There is no middle ground for these people. But life isn't black or white. Life is ambiguous with many right answers. Creativity lives in the gray areas—in the mixing and matching of ideas.

- **Self-Fulfilling Prophecy**

  A self-inflicted box is the self-fulfilling prophecy. You're locked in when you tell yourself that you are not a creative person. We become what we think. Period. Visualizing success is a well-accepted technique used by many Olympic teams and successful athletes in golf, football, basketball, swimming, skiing, skating and track. What do they know that could make you more successful? If you see yourself inventing new ideas, developing innovative solutions and being creative, you will fulfill your expectation. Henry Ford said, "whether you think you can or can't, you'll prove yourself correct."

- **Bottom-Line Thinking**

  No one in business would dare not respect the bottom line. The bottom-line thinking box traps you by insisting that creativity wastes money. These people have not learned from their company's creative past. They do not see their company's creative present. They will not support their company's creative future. Companies must constantly innovate and improve to stay ahead of their competition. Innovation begins with an idea in someone's mind.

- **Environmental Pollution**

  Your working environment does have an influence on you. A few people put themselves into the environmental pollution box by insisting that they do not work in a creative environment. They list noise level, a lack of privacy, no windows or no reward as reasons that inhibit their creativity. They see creativity as sparked from outside of themselves. They have not tapped their inner resources.

- **Only One Right Answer**

  The only one right answer box is holding those who believe that there exists only one correct answer to a problem. They stop at the first right answer they find and cheat themselves of creative answers. This not only prevents more creative answers, but also prevents them from learning and growing.

- **Calm Waters**

  For some people, the waters must be calm in order for business to operate effectively and efficiently. There can be no rocking the boat. These people are shut into the calm waters box. They fear being different and perceive their creativity as making waves. Both the organization and the individual are cheated because creativity never bubbles up. These folks are masters at stating and hearing killer phrases such as, "that will never work," or "we tried that last year."

 ASK if participants have identified their boxes—those attitudes that keep them in the dark and prevent them from being as creative as they could be?

 SAY that you would like them to spend the next 30 minutes working in pairs or trios with others who have identified the same uncreative boxes as you. The five page handout entitled *Unbox Your Creativity* (pp. 143-147) match the *Nine Uncreative Boxes*. They should find someone and do the activity stated for one or two of the boxes.

SAY: During this activity you will explore how to get out of your boxes—how to unbox your creativity and bring it into the light.

There is time flexibility within this activity. If you are short of time, participants can address only one box. If you have ample time they can complete up to three activities.

Be sure to save 20 minutes at the end to debrief the activity so that small groups can share some of their ideas.

After 30 minutes, bring the group together and ask the pairs and trios to share some of their discoveries. You may use the following information for each of the activities in any way you wish to guide the discussion.

This information is here to provide ideas and insight to the exercises. Usually the participants will have more and better information to share as a result of their activity. In addition, realize that all of the boxes may not be discussed, if they weren't chosen by the individuals.

Option

Use the following as supplemental information:

Tear Apart Time Trapped Boxes!

One easy way to tear this box to shreds is to identify new time-frames for doing your creative work.

Most of us are creative during unusual times, in the shower, mowing the lawn, jogging, driving or walking to work, for example. We have creative thoughts when we are relaxed, in our right brain (yes, driving has become a right brain activity for most of us!). During running or exercise, our brain produces endorphins, which account for a runner's high. But endorphins, an opiate-like substance that produces a euphoric high, also enhance our ability to be creative. The key is to capture these creative bursts of ideas when they occur. The problem isn't finding time to be creative. Instead it is taking time to capture your creative ideas.

Rip the Risky Business Zone!

Ask one of the participants to share a recent risk. Have two or three others share their experiences. Discuss how sharing their experiences was a risk. Ask the group how the cliché, "Nothing ventured; nothing gained," portrays the role of risk taking in the business world.

To be on the leading edge demands risk taking. Only corporations with vision and risk-taking skills will survive.

You may wish to discuss the quotation found at the bottom of the page, "There is no likelihood man can ever tap the power of the atom," by Robert Millkan (1868–1953, American physicist).

Perforate the Perfectionist's Problem!

Poking holes in the perfectionist's problem is no easy job. It takes courage and determination to go against the grain. Many successful people are burdened with an overdose of perfectionism. There are two locks on the perfectionist box. One has to do with fear of not being perfect. The other is related to not knowing when the goal has been met.

P

Pinpoint your goal!

First, make sure that you know what you are trying to achieve. Define it as objectively and as concretely as you can. Visualize it. Be clear.

E

Examine alternatives!

Review all of the ways you can achieve your goal. If you do not examine the alternatives, you will not find the "best" method.

R

Reach out for it!

The third step is to DO something or you will be stuck in refining and researching. To break the perfectionist's problem, you must ACT.

F

Feel to verify if you've found it!

Use your intuition or gut-level feelings to assess your status with the project. If it "feels right," do it! Don't waste time perfecting!

E

Evaluate your progress!

The key word here is progress: did you perform the first four steps? If so, you have progressed.

C

Congratulate your effort!

Reward yourself for your progress. The positive reinforcement will help you to break the perfectionist's problem of fear of failure.

T

Try again!

If you are not satisfied with the results simply try again. Do not chastise yourself, or quit, or become locked into the perfectionist's box.

Perfectionist behavior locks in your creativity. Only you can free it by trying to follow these steps. You don't need to be perfect (adjective) to perfect (verb).

Suggested responses to the phrases at the bottom of the page may include:

- To try is—progress, success.

- Making a mistake is—trying, learning.

- Falling short of the goal is —success, progress and trying.

Remember, Thomas Edison knew 1800 ways how not to make a light bulb.

End Wright or Wrong Thinking!

You have learned to make decisions, and you are responsible for the results of those decisions. You have learned to think on your feet and to act quickly. These skills are important to you and to your company. This cannot be diminished. However, one word of caution. Such demanding decisions can cause people to become locked into the wright or wrong thinking box.

When was the last time you should have asked a "what if" to your wright or wrong thinking? Trust your judgment, but do not allow it to lock you into this box.

Don't set rules; your decisions will be based on such rules. (e.g., "I have to attend that meeting," "I can't eat dessert first," "I must get eight hours of sleep.") You don't have to do anything, except live with the consequences of your decisions.

Empty the Self-Fulfilling Prophecy!

We can be our own worst enemy. This is especially apparent in the case of the self-fulfilling prophecy.

The subconscious mind cannot distinguish between the "real" and the imagined. Visualization is a strong teacher. One of the first studies that provided insight into the self-fulfilling prophecy was conducted at a well known university. Volunteer students were divided into three groups and rated according to their ability to make basketball free-throws. The first group, the control group was told to do nothing for the next two weeks. The second group practiced free-throws for 20 minutes every day for two weeks. The third group was told not to touch a basketball, but to visualize themselves making free-throws with 100% accuracy. There was no change in the control group. The second group increased its average by 24%. The third group improved its average by 23% without touching a ball. The moral? See yourself successful and you will be. See yourself creative and you are. Whether you think you can or cannot, you will prove yourself correct.

ASK participants to say outloud together ten times the phrase, "I am creative."

Ask them to say this to themselves ten times once a day to "program" their subconscious. Make the point that the messages they give themselves strengthen the neuron bridges in the brain.

Bust Bottom-Line Thinking!

The bottom line for any business is profit. Period. People only buy what they want or need. Period. The question that this box raises is, "What place does creativity have in making a profit?"

Arthur Pedrick was the world's most unsuccessful inventor. He patented 162 inventions from 1962–1977, and even more since then. None were ever produced commercially. For example, he created:

- A bike with amphibious capacity.

- A car attachment that enables a person to drive from the back seat.

- A golf ball that can be steered in flight.

These are all very creative—but did not result in innovative products. Why did these fail? Because the self-interest of the creator and the interest of the user conflicted. Innovation is creativity made usable. Innovation meets the user's needs, your customer's or client's needs.

Pull Apart Environmental Pollution!

Discuss what elements in an environment could stifle or box creativity. Make the following points:

- **Décor**

  Some people are more affected by color than others. If the environment is drab, these people feel dull and uncreative.

- **Noises**

  Many people are distracted by noise in the workplace. For others, they need noise in order to work more effectively.

- **Alone time**

  In today's offices, shutting out the world is neither possible nor advisable. Interruptions by phone and face-to-face contact can distract some people.

- **Attitudes of others**

  This may be the single most influential element in the environment. How creative endeavors are perceived by co-workers and especially superiors has a meaningful impact on the working environment.

Find out what works for you and include these things in your environment.

Eliminate Only One Right Answer!

After working for several hours, sometimes days, to reach a solution or answer to a particular problem, it is easy to accept the first answer that you find. Often people become so committed to that hard-earned answer that they cannot see alternatives. The problem with only one right answer is that it boxes in other creative ideas.

Ripple Calm Waters!

One business rule that continues to drown creativity is the idea that one should not make waves. It warns that it is important to pull together and to not make changes, suggestions, remarks or proposals that would ripple the calm, collected, efficient waters of the company. This attitude has merit in that anarchy will destroy any organization. However, if this attitude stops the flow of creative ideas, the company will run aground.

It is important to APPROPRIATELY ripple the calm waters. You know the appropriate procedures for implementing such changes in your organization. Use them to make your suggestions.

Debrief   *SUMMARIZE* the entire activity by saying that these boxes prevent each of us from being creative. We need to do two things:

- Recognize how we box ourselves in and prevent the flow of creativity.

- Practice pushing ourselves out of the boxes using some of the ideas we have just discussed.

Options You may:

- Use the overhead for this activity.

- Assign different groups to each of the boxes if your objective is to cover all of the boxes.

Notes
- _____
- _____
- _____
- _____
- _____
- _____
- _____
- _____

<u>TRAINER'S NOTES</u>	**Color-Blind Energizer**
Objective	To provide a quick energizer between activities of any kind, to introduce a very simple right-brain thinking activity and the idea of working together to multiply ideas. This activity can be used as a warm up to a brainstorming session.
	This activity is taken from the set of *Idea Sparkers* described in the appendix (p. 291). You may have a set of *Idea Sparkers* available for them to look for other ways to "spark their creativity."
Time	• 10 minutes.
Materials	• Paper and pencil.

Procedure

1. To introduce the activity, *SAY*:

   It is important to exercise your mind. You can strengthen your creativity skills, by reading creative books, visiting unusual places (like a toy store when you really have no toys to purchase), reading magazines outside your profession, using creativity tools or other creativity enhancing activities. If you practice making the shift from left-brain to right-brain thinking daily, you will strengthen your ability to be creative when you need to come up with new ideas.

2. *ASK* them to take out a piece of paper and pencil (or crayon) and have them list as many shades of green (e.g., olive, grass, pine, lime) as they can in three minutes.

3. Have them work two minutes with a partner.

4. Find out how many shades each team listed.

5. Have volunteers share some of their responses (the most common, most unique, ugliest).

6. Ask what happened when you worked with partners?

Debrief

To summarize this activity, *ASK*: What does this say about creativity?

Facilitate the responses to include:

• Two heads are better than one.

• Concept of "building on" others' ideas to create new ones.

• Many of us need stimuli to enhance our own creativity.

TRAINER'S NOTES   **My Creative Climate**

Objective   To introduce the concept that the environment affects an individual's ability to be creative and to help participants explore the kind of environment they need personally to be creative.

Time   • 20 minutes.

Materials   • Handout *My Creative Climate* (p. 149).

Procedure 1. ***INTRODUCE*** this activity by saying that our environment can affect our ability to be creative. In this activity we will turn our attention to building the type of environment that encourages and rewards creative efforts. Add some interesting facts by saying:

Most creative people understand the need for a specific environment or routine that enhances their creative abilities. Some famous people have shared what "keeps their creative juices flowing." For example:

• Mozart (18th–century Austrian composer) needed to exercise before he composed music.

• Dr. Samuel Johnson (18–century English author) wanted a purring cat, orange peels and tea in his creative environment.

• Immanuel Kant (German philosopher) liked to work in bed at times with blankets arranged in a special way.

• Hart Crane (20th–century American poet) played jazz loudly on a Victrola.

• Johann Schiller (18th–century German poet) needed to fill his desk with rotten apples.

• Archimedes (ancient Greek mathematician and inventor) recognized the importance of relaxing and often solved his most difficult problems in a hot bath.

• Samuel Cray of super-computer fame, digs a tunnel beneath his house when he feels blocked from creative ideas.

Get in touch with what makes you feel creative. Is it certain scents (the change of seasons, cinnamon, baking bread), sights (sunrises, mountains, vacation pictures, flowers), sounds (ocean waves, jazz music, silence), tastes (chocolate, oranges, cappuccino) or feels (cool glass, a comfortable sweatshirt, a spring breeze)? What makes you feel more creative?

2. **REFER** participants to the *My Creative Climate* handout (p. 149). Share your own creative climate needs as an example. Jot them down here before the session.

My creative climate needs are:

* _____

* _____

* _____

* _____

* _____

* _____

* _____

* _____

* _____

* _____

* _____

3. **TELL** participants to take five minutes to complete their *My Creative Climate* handout.

4. **SHARE** ideas as a large group.

Debrief

SUMMARIZE this activity by saying that it is important to know what stimuli triggers, as well as prevents, our creativity. The more environmental factors we can have in place that enhance our ability to be creative, the easier it will be to create new ideas.

<u>**TRAINER'S NOTES**</u>   **Take a Risk**

Objective   To explore the idea of risk taking and to identify ways to take risks appropriately and to encourage risk taking in others.

This activity requires time outside of your workshop. Participants need either a lunch period or an evening to complete their risks.

Time
- 45 minutes in the session, plus time to take a risk (lunch or evening if a two-day program).

Materials
- *Turtle Awards* (p. 289).
- Handout *Risky Business* (p. 151).
- Overhead *Turtle Race* (p. 274).

Procedure

1. At the appropriate time in the session introduce the activity by *SAYING:*

   I'd like you to take a risk. You may define "risk" in any way that you choose. You should be prepared to report back about your risk. If you think you will do something unbelievable, take the *Risky Business* handout (p. 151) and have a witness sign it.

2. Following the allotted time for taking the risk, take 20 minutes to discuss the risks people took. Facilitate the discussion, allowing everyone who wishes to share what they did with the group. You may ask:

   - How many of you took a risk?
   - How do the risks differ?
   - Are some risks less-risky? More calculated? Crazier?
   - Why do you suppose that is true?
   - Is it important to take risks?

3. *REFER* to the *Turtle Race* overhead (p. 274).

   - Assuming that it is important for your organization to encourage appropriate risk taking, have the participants form groups of five. Give them ten minutes in their groups to identify what should be done to take appropriate risks and what can be done to encourage risk taking in others.

   - Bring the group together and use a round robin to have the small groups share their ideas. Post these ideas on a flipchart.

Debrief   *CLOSE* this activity by providing *Turtle Awards* for the risk takers.

TRAINER'S NOTES   A Spectrum of Creativity Technique s

Objective

To introduce participants to ten creativity techniques and to provide participants with an opportunity to practice one of the techniques.

Time

- 90–120 minutes.

Materials

- Handout *A Spectrum of Creativity Techniques* (p. 150).

- Handouts *Your Creative Spectrum* (pp. 152-162).

- Overhead *A Spectrum Of Creativity Techniques* (p. 273).

- Trainer's script *Ten Idea-Generating Techniques* (pp. 219-222).

- Group table tents (pp. 284-288) placed on tables before the session begins.

- Crayons.

- Play-Doh.

Procedure

1. *HAVE* participants turn to *A Spectrum of Creativity Techniques* handout.

2. *USE* the overhead, *A Spectrum of Creativity Techniques* (p. 273) and the revealing method to uncover each technique as you speak about it. This will help your participants stay focused.

3. *ASK* them to jot down a few notes as you briefly explain each of the techniques. Encourage them to ask questions along the way to clarify your comments. The script begins on page 219.

4. Take 30–40 minutes to describe the rationale behind the ten idea-generating techniques and give examples.

5. Have participants turn to the *Your Creative Spectrum* handouts.

SAY that you would like them to work in small groups. Once they reach their small group they should decide which of the ten techniques they would like to practice. If time permits, they may complete two activities. Once in their small group they will have a total of 30 minutes. They should select a technique and complete the activity as addressed on the specific technique page.

6.   *TELL* them the following instructions to divide them into five small groups.

There are five table tents (*Is a closet poet*, *Would like to write a book*, *Enjoys daydreaming*, *Likes to play with clay*, *Has painted a picture*) around the room. Select the area that most represents you and go to that spot.

Once there are _____ people in a group, move to your second choice. (Establish a maximum number in each group. For example, if you have 18 people, you might say, "no more than four people in a group; after four people are in a group, move to your second choice.")

7.   *MONITOR* the groups:

- Move from group to group making sure they each know what they are to do.

- Circulate a couple of times to answer questions or keep them on track.

8.   *CALL* time, giving two signals. Announce that their time is half over after about 15 minutes. Also, announce when five minutes of their time is left so they can begin to wrap up.

Debrief   To close the activity, bring the participants back together as a large group to discover what each group did and what they learned.

ASK each group to report their ideas.

Watch the time closely to ensure that each team has time to report.

Options   If you want every technique discussed, divide the participants into ten teams and assign each a technique. Recognize that it will take twice as much time to debrief the activity.

You may use each of the techniques separately within other workshops to generate ideas.

Notes

- _____
- _____
- _____
- _____
- _____

Ten Idea-Generating Techniques

1. Compare and combine

These are actually two different techniques but both have to do with putting together different concepts.

Compare is the use of similes and metaphors to explore a topic, problem or idea. How is creativity like a blizzard? Training like suspenders? The compare technique was used to invent Pringle Potato Chips. What's the biggest problem with potato chips? Preventing breakage in packaging. So, Pringles said, "How is a potato chip like a leaf?" And when doesn't that leaf break? When it has moisture within it. The concept of shaping and packaging Pringles while still moist came about because of this exploratory technique. This technique provides a fresh perspective and gets you to question assumptions.

Combine is a force-fit technique which brings different elements together in unique ways. What happens if you combine a wine press and a coin punch? Gutenberg invented the printing press. What happens if you combine a refrigerator and a railroad car? Swift invented the refrigerated railroad car. What happens if you combine rubber and a waffle iron? Bill Bowerman discovered a sole for his Nike shoe.

2. Risk taking

The year Babe Ruth hit the most home runs, he also struck out the most often. What does this suggest? Perhaps to "go for the big one" we need to take bigger risks. Successful people must be comfortable with risk. How we are treated as risk takers who fail (Babe Ruth, Thomas Edison) will impact a willingness to try again. Do you celebrate your failures as well as your successes? Tom Peters says that failure is a sign someone is doing something! He also says companies should "fail faster!" Get the failures (trials) out of the way so they can go on to the "big ones!" Creative people tend to make more mistakes. Creativity without risk is just an embryonic thought, an idea without action.

3. Expand and shrink

This technique is the process of blowing an idea (conceptual level) or object (physical level) out of proportion or shrinking it down to a smaller scale. For example, you could expand the idea of window curtains to stage drapes or shrink them down to a camera shutter. Take your department's most recent problem and ask, "What if this was a problem for the entire company?" or "What if this problem belonged to a three year old?" What would be different?

Has anyone ever plucked a chicken? First you plunge the chicken into scalding water for a few seconds to loosen the feathers for plucking. What's left after the feathers are gone? Hair. And how do you get that hair off the chicken? You singe it. But since you have a wet chicken, the hairs won't always burn. How could you dry that chicken quickly? Frank Perdue of Perdue Chicken fame asked that question. A hair dryer, of course. But when you have thousands of birds to dry that seems like a very small tool for a very large job. What do you get when you expand a hair dryer? A jet engine!

4. Ask what's good? and what if?

These questions are critical to opening up our creative vision. What's good about a flood? What's good about being fired? What's good about toxic waste? Engineers at Conoco asked that question and discovered a substance in the water that could be turned into a lubricant.

What if we found the magic potent that allowed all of us to live to be 200? What if the problem was actually worse—what would it look like? What if our problems were actually our solutions? What if we paid more money to fewer vendors? DuPont Information Systems asked that question and saved $400,000.

Ask the questions. It's a wonderful technique that will get you through many problems and issues at work and at home.

5. Transform your viewpoint

This technique can be used in many different ways. First, transform your viewpoint to someone else. Ask how would the following see this problem: The CEO? Your secretary? The customer? A kindergartner? A magician? Winnie the Pooh?

What if you transformed your viewpoint to another time? How would this problem have been handled in 1897? How will it be handled in 2010? How would it be handled the first year the company opened?

You may also transform your viewpoint from negative to positive or positive to negative. For example, if you were trying to develop a better way to motivate employees to be creative, ask, "How could we de-motivate employees' creative efforts?" Seeing the other side can be a very valuable tool.

You may also transform your viewpoint by changing the circumstances. How would you approach the idea (or problem) if: Money were no object? If you were a genius? If you had only 30 days to live? If you were the CEO? If the company moved to Hawaii?

6. In another sequence

This technique suggests that you explore other sequences:

• What if you did the steps in the process in a different order?

• What if you did the process backward?

• What if you looked at the problem backward?

• What if the problem was actually the solution?

In the insurance industry, what if you got death benefits before you died? Prudential came up with the living benefit life insurance. It pays death benefits to people who are suffering terminal illness before they die.

7. Visit other places

Where do you go to get creative ideas? Many people just go for a walk. Most of us need stimuli to encourage the budding of creative thoughts. Try visiting some of these places to get a new idea, a fresh perspective or just a heavy dose of stimuli: toy store, hike in the mountains, ocean, walk along the lake shore, zoo, woods, meadow, farm, book store, large magazine store, car ride in the country, lying in your backyard on a starry night, lunch with a friend, long soaking bath in your bathtub, art gallery, museum, movie, New York, library, factory, candy store, housewares store, hardware store, sunset, sunrise, park or any other personally stimulating place.

8. Incubate

Remember when you were in school and your English teacher tried to encourage you to write your report early so that you could "put it on the back burner"? She was actually helping you tap into your subconscious, where your creative sparks really fly!

The incubate technique simply means that after you have gathered data and information and have reviewed it, you let it sit and gurgle in your brain. It needs to simmer on the back burner to let your creative juices work. This is the time to do something else, something unrelated to your idea. Or, try sleeping or dreaming on it.

Have you ever awakened in the middle of the night with the perfect solution to a problem. You knew it was too good to forget, but by morning you did forget it! How can you make your dreams work for you?

1. Before you go to sleep, think about the problem. Think about it like a metaphor. The subconscious likes metaphors.

2. Just before falling asleep, give yourself a mental suggestion that you will remember what you dream.

3. When you awake, don't open your eyes, since the stimuli will immediately wipe out the memory of your dream. Instead, review the dream.

4. Open your eyes and immediately write it down. It helps to keep a pen and paper (or tape recorder) by your bed with light available. (There are some lighted note pads and pens made just for this purpose.)

5. In the morning, review your dreams, looking for patterns and reoccurrences.

Why does this work? Your conscious mind can focus on only one idea at a time. Your subconscious, however can focus on several at once. It allows your mind to wander and connect ideas that are floating around.

Looking for creative ideas? Perhaps the best you can do is to "give it a break!"

6. Trigger concepts

This technique can be personalized easily. Some people have a "shopping list" of their favorite words (serendipity, daydreaming, waves, clouds, dancing, autumn, golf, snow, bistro, birds of paradise, hot tub, avocado, destiny, hot fudge sundaes) which they will use to free associate with the issue at hand. Others use a preposition list (about, among, before, behind, beyond, despite, except, on, outside, under, with) in the same way.

Some people keep creativity files in which they keep items (favorite pictures, creative articles, cartoons, jokes, sayings, proverbs, quotes, creative advertisements) that stimulate their creative juices.

Author, Richard Bach, introduced us to a similar technique. Put your dilemma in the form of a question. Then pull out a favorite book and without looking, open the book to any page and point to any passage. Connect the meaning of the passage to the dilemma. You can do the same with a dictionary or newspaper. Force fit the word you select to your situation.

You may also use objects. Look around your office. Select an item. How could that item solve your problem or add life to your idea? For example, let's say you were trying to improve the bathtub. Look around the room and select an item. What improvement can you create?

7. Youth's advantage

This technique asks you to get in touch with the child inside. Look for the fun in the problem. Your brain is more likely to create new ideas when you're having fun.

Certain childlike mental operations are essential to creativity, including playfulness, wishfulness, spontaneity, stimulation, pretending, daydreaming and free-association of ideas.

Why do you suppose I have placed crayons and Play-Doh on the table in front of you? To stimulate your creativity; to get you to loosen up! Look at your problem through the eyes of a child. A child is curious, asking lots of "why" questions. A child will look for the fun in it. A child will approach it innocently and without inhibitions. Play with some of your child's toys.

You might also try to interview a child about the situation. How does the child see your problem? Remember a recent NASA space telescope problem was solved while the scientist was playing with his child's Tinkertoys.

TRAINER'S NOTES	**Road to Success**
Objective	To help participants see how companies and schools may inadvertently inhibit creativity, and to explore what individuals can do to encourage a more creative climate in organizations.

Time
- 45–90 minutes.

Materials
- Handout *Opened Climates* (pp. 167-168).
- Overhead *Where Can Creativity Flourish?* (p. 276).
- Trainer's script *Road to Success* (pp. 225-232).
- Crayons.
- Clay.
- Play-Doh (or other quiet manipulative toys).
- Slides (optional; see Appendix p. 292).

Procedure

1. *INTRODUCE* this activity by saying: I'm going to read a short story (or show a slide presentation) to you. During that time please feel free to color, shape clay, doodle or just sit back and imagine this happening in this city, in this company, in your department, to you.

2. *READ* the *Road to Success* script and show the slides if available. Follow by asking questions to initiate a discussion.

   - How did you feel at the end of the story? (Expect to hear depressed, upset, angry.)
   - Can you think of other examples or experiences where creativity is snuffed out?

3. *FACILITATE* a discussion, allowing the participants to make the following points:

   - It can be difficult to foster our own, let alone others' creativity. Yet, it is so easy to squash and even punish creativity in those we touch.
   - An awareness of what creativity is and how it can be nurtured will help us avoid pushing everyone down the tried and true road to success as depicted in the story.

4. *SAY:* Let's spend a few minutes examining what we as individuals can do to encourage a more creative climate. What are some positive steps we can take as an organization?

5. *PROVIDE* each participant with the *Opened Climates* handout. Explain that these six factors have been found to be imperative to creating a climate that is open to creative expression. The handout provides several ideas for each of the factors.

6. *HAVE* participants organize themselves into six groups. Assign one of the categories—Open-minded, Perceptive, Equal, Nurturing, Encouraging and Descriptive—to each of the teams. Have them take 15–25 minutes to expand on these ideas or list others of their own.

7. After the groups have completed the task, *ASK* the six groups to report the ideas they discussed.

As participants are discussing their ideas, you may list them on the overhead, *Where Can Creativity Flourish?* (p. 276).

ASK: How many of these can we do as a company?

Debrief

SUMMARIZE by asking volunteers to state which of these are most appealing to them and which they will try to implement.

Road to Success Philosophy

The purpose of this (slide) presentation is to allow participants to discover the ways that creativity can be squelched and to feel that loss. Its story is an allegory with fictional characters that represent all people, young and old. Through their symbolic actions and reactions generalized truths about the loss of creativity are illustrated. These characters are "larger than life" exaggerations of the norm.

The spirit of creativity is represented as a flower throughout the presentation:

1. A child draws a flower which does not conform. It is criticized and rejected.

2. The child hides the rejected flower.

3. The child creates a flower like everyone else's. Creativity is rejected by the child.

• Read the script with feeling. Practice reading aloud until you are satisfied with its tone.

• If you are using the slides, a flower "❀" is placed at advancement points beside the text that is to be read with that particular slide.

Option

To add meaning to this presentation, have the participants create a flower of their own before you read the script.

TRAINER'S SCRIPT   **Road to Success Script**

The story takes about five minutes to read, and poignantly uncovers why children as well as adults, individuals as well as companies, are boxed in and unable to use all their creative potential.

You will probably want to practice reading the story aloud several times before you present it.

Slides for the story are available, but definitely not necessary. They are listed in the appendix on page 292.

❁ (Title slide)

❁ (Credit slide)

❁ (ebb press logo)

❁ As often happens in the world of business,

A bright, creative man earned a promotion.

He'd been the Director of a regional branch for three years.

And his new responsibilities and position

Seemed stressful and a bit scary.

The relocation to the Corporate Headquarters

Presented a substantial change for him and his family.

❁ However, once he was established,

The bright man discovered

That even though his new office was larger

And his authority had broader limits,

His staff members were friendly

And his boss was supportive.

He was well pleased.

And the new position and relocation

Didn't seem quite so stressful anymore.

❁ One day, after he'd been in the new position for a while,

His boss said, "We need to initiate cost-saving changes.

We think you are just the man,

To head up the project and meet the challenge."

✿ The creative man was happy; he admired his boss.

He relished challenges and liked initiating changes.

Many times he'd developed new ideas for the regional branch.

He'd piloted the company's Customer Service Program.

And his office had been the first to use Flexible Hours.

✿ Anxious to get started,

He entered his office and began to consider alternatives.

He worked furiously for the rest of the day,

And part of the next morning, too.

Then, as was his custom,

He placed his brainstormed ideas on a backburner,

And he turned to more routine tasks.

✿ Later that week, the boss came to the man's office

And he questioned the man about the project.

"Well, how's it going? What do you have to offer?"

The boss spoke with enthusiasm and anticipation.

Proudly, the man shared his brainstorming ideas

And mapped out his alternative solutions,

Saying he'd need more time to complete the assignment.

✿ "Wait a minute," the boss interrupted.

"I didn't ask for maybe's and could be's

We need answers—and now!"

The man sat back in his chair puzzled by his boss's angry tone.

He admired the boss and wanted to please him.

"You've got to learn how to solve problems like our other V.P.s.

That has been our road to success.

Try again, but do it right this time."

✿ The boss left, shaking his head.

And the man placed his rejected ideas in a bottom drawer of his desk.

❁ Soon after he began the important project,

The man visited his son's school room.

As a loving father of a young boy,

He was proud to view a drawing that his son had done.

It was a flower in full bloom,

And it stood out from the others displayed.

He also knew that his son had worked hard on a book report due that day.

❁ As he observed the class, he overheard the teacher remarking,

"What you've done in your report is all right.

But, we write reports differently here.

Please redo your book report so it's like all the others.

And you'll want to change your flower, too.

It has a blue, not green, stem.

And it's not like the others.

The petals should be yellow, you know."

The boy liked his teacher,

He wanted to follow her instructions.

His father watched him take down his flower.

❁ Later that evening at the dinner table,

The man spoke with his son about the report.

"I understand your report wasn't acceptable.

Learn to do it the teacher's way.

That will be your road to success."

His son sat silently and listened.

The boy loved and respected his dad.

"Try again, son, but do it right this time," the father said.

"And work on your flower, too."

❁ After supper, the boy tore up his old report,

And threw the pieces away.

He didn't tear up the flower, though.

He hung it inside his closet door.

✿   The next morning,

The man was asked to meet with a Committee.

His boss told the man that this Committee would help.

It could lead the man to the Company Way.

The man liked to try new approaches.

He enjoyed learning new things.

So he entered the meeting positively.

✿   The agenda was set in black and white.

And the Chair of the Committee said it would be followed.

No additions or amendments were allowed.

The man waited to learn.

He admired and respected his peers.

Proposals and motions were made.

The man thought some were on target.

✿   Others, he questioned.

He explored colorful alternatives and asked "what ifs."

Each time he tried to do so,

A fellow member of the Committee would help him.

✿   "We don't do things that way here.

We deal in black and white,

It's our tried and true road to success.

That's the Company Way."

✿   At first the man asked more questions.

He tried to find out why and to explore the spectrum of ideas.

But then, each member's response began to leave its black mark,

He was learning the Company Way.

He was a bright man.

Although he still liked some of his colorful ideas better.

That night the man helped his son.

The boy had brought home the teacher's rules.

Together they worked on the new book report.

The boy loved his father.

And the boy liked to try new things.

"Can't I paint the picture of the characters?"

The boy enjoyed using his watercolors.

"No. These rules say to use ink only."

The man helped his boy.

 "Why can't I tell what I hated about the book?"

"Because, Son, it says to tell why you liked it."

"Can't I use the computer to word process it?"

"It says 'handwritten' here," his dad replied.

"I thought I'd take my cassette player, Dad.

I want to play some music used during the character's time period."

"You only have five minutes, Son.

Use it wisely; follow the teacher's way."

 Carefully, they reviewed all the rules.

The boy worked hard to follow them.

At last, the report was completed.

The boy didn't like it much,

He thought it dull.

But his father liked it.

And he wanted to please his dad.

In the week that followed,

The man toiled over his project work.

He spent countless hours writing and rewriting.

Keeping in mind, all the time,

The advice of the Committee.

❀   Once in awhile he found himself

Slipping into the old habit of questioning,

Trying to explore the kaleidoscope of ideas.

But, being well disciplined,

He repressed these urges.

And he pressed for the untainted truth.

As a final check,

The man ran the proposal

Past a few members of the Committee.

❀   It was returned with many comments.

"Don't try this; it's too radical, too off-color."

"Good! This has been successful for years!"

"It's logical, black and white."

"You've almost got it, the Company Way."

The man revised the proposal using the comments,

And, at last, he was done.

He didn't really like the finished product.

But, tomorrow was his deadline.

❀   He submitted it a day early.

He wanted to exceed his boss' expectations.

❀   Driving home from work,

The man thought about his new position.

He felt more comfortable now.

He had more confidence in himself.

Silently, he admitted that the Committee,

In its wisdom, had helped him indeed.

It had been much easier to do this project.

Much easier than any he had tried before.

Why, he didn't feel stressed at all!

❀ He felt—comfortably calm; grayly quiet.

He was certain he was on the road to success.

There was, of course, no thrill, or electric excitement.

But, maybe he'd been too hard on himself before.

All other times after completing a project,

He'd felt so vibrant, so much alive and filled with color.

That was probably too stressful a way to work.

The Company Way felt more comfortable, more stable.

❀ He picked his son up from basketball practice,

And he asked him about the book report.

"We got them back today; I got an 'A'."

"Great! See how well you did?"

The father clasped his son's shoulder.

"How do you feel, now, about the teacher's way?"

The boy sat quietly for a moment.

"Okay, I guess. I really don't feel anything about it."

"That's how it should be, you know."

The father explained gently.

"It's more comfortable that way, Son."

❀ The boy loved and respected his father.

But he wouldn't tell him about the new science project.

It would be no problem.

He wouldn't need his dad's help on it.

He knew the road to success now.

It was the teacher's way.

❀ Early the next morning,

The boss called the man into his office.

"Sit down. Sit down. We need to talk,"

The boss began the conversation.

"Well, I've reviewed your proposal.

I've sent it to others at my level for comment.

I can see that the Committee did its work."

The man sat and listened; he respected his boss.

"I want to congratulate you!
You've found it—the Company Way.
You're on the road to success."
And the boss shook the man's hand
"Now, we have another project for you.
But, we want you to be creative with it.
This one concerns the quality of our employees' work lives.
You handled the last project so well.
Have fun on the road to success."
And he heard the details about his new project.
He took many notes; but he asked no questions.

🌼 He left the office calmly that evening.
He didn't feel excited, he felt nothing.
The new project wasn't really a challenge,
It was just a different subject to process.
He wouldn't go to work on it immediately.
He realized that he didn't need to get started right away.
After all, he now knew the road to success.
It was the Company Way.

🌼 Once at home, he thought he'd chat with his son.
Stepping into the boy's room,
The father noticed a drawing lying on his son's desk.
Walking over to view the colorful work,
The father smiled a proud smile.
His son had learned to draw a flower.
He had drawn it the teacher's way.
He was on the road to success

🌼 The flower was perfect.
The stem was green.
It's petals, yellow.

🌼 (last flower slide)

🌼 (blank slide)

TRAINER'S NOTES	**Killer Phrases**

Objective

To identify phrases that kill creative or new ideas and to put in their places phrases that encourage creativity.

Time

- 25–35 minutes.

Materials

- Handout *Killer Phrases* (p. 169) or blank paper.

Procedure

1. *STATE* that killer phrases, found in the culture of many organizations, are some of the things that prevent creative ideas from bubbling to the surface.

2. *HAVE* participants take a clean sheet of paper and individually list as many phrases as they can think of that have stopped an idea. Give them some to get started:

   - It won't work!

   - We tried that last year!

   - That's not the way we do things!

   - We're not quite ready for that!

   - It's not practical!

   - Top management will never go for it!

   - Ideas are a dime a dozen!

3. Allow four to six minutes for this listing.

4. *SAY:* those phrases get hurled around everyday. So let's hurl them a couple last times. Wad up that piece of paper and toss it at someone here.

5. Once they have all tossed their pages, suggest that they do it once more.

   SAY: let's see what some of those missiles say. Everyone needs to have one of the paper balls. Let's read some of your phrases. Get a couple people started reading one or two phrases from the pages they have. Create chaos by encouraging everyone to read them faster and louder at the same time.

6. At the end, exclaim, "that's quite a list!"

   I think the least we can do is get rid of all creativity killer phrases. Set the wastebasket in the middle of the room and have them wad up the page one last time and toss the killer phrases away for good.

7. *ASK:* now that we've eliminated the killer phrases, what do we put in their place?

As a large group brainstorm a list of encouragers—phrases that support and encourage new ideas. To get them started:

- Nice job!

- Tell me how that would work!

- What do you need to move forward?

- Where else could we use that?

- You make the decision.

- Go for it!

8. Conduct this brainstorming for 10–15 minutes.

Debrief

SUMMARIZE this activity by saying that it is very easy to discourage new ideas by what we say and how we say it. To foster a creative culture, we need to increase the use of encouragers and eliminate the use of killer phrases.

Notes

- _____
- _____
- _____
- _____
- _____
- _____
- _____
- _____
- _____
- _____
- _____
- _____
- _____
- _____
- _____
- _____

TRAINER'S NOTES

Thumbprints Energizer

Objective

To allow participants to tap into their right brain, to provide an energizer between activities and to discuss the rules that sometimes prevent us from doing unusual things.

Time

- 10–20 minutes.

Materials

- Paper ink pads (and disposable towelettes for clean-up).

- Tape deck.

- Cassettes of wild, dramatic or fun music (optional). (This activity is more fun if accompanied by background music.)

Procedure

1. *PROVIDE* ink pads for each table or one pad for every three to four people. Have participants press their thumbs on the pads and put their thumbprints any place on their participant materials or on a blank piece of paper.

2. *ASK* them to make their thumbprints into something (e.g., a bug, a car, a flying saucer, etc.) Let them play for a few minutes.

3. *HAVE* them share their creations with the large group.

4. *FACILITATE* a discussion by asking some of the following questions:

   - What were your first thoughts when you learned about the activity?

   - How did you feel doing the activity?

   - Have you ever made thumbprint pictures? What was the occasion?

   - Why might some people not like to do this?

   - What rules might you or others have that would prevent you from enjoying this activity?

   - What is the benefit of this activity?

Debrief

CLOSE this activity by stating that many people may have created rules that prevent them from enjoying activities like this. The benefit is that the activity is good for forcing right-brain thinking. And more than that, it is useful for pushing us outside our boxes.

TRAINER'S NOTES   **Brainstorming Plans for Personal Creativity**

Objective   To identify steps participants can take to be more creative.

Time
- 30–40 minutes.

Materials
- Handout *Brainstorming* (pp. 171-172).
- Overhead *Brainstorming* (p. 277).
- Flipcharts.
- Pens.
- Masking tape.

Procedure

1. *INTRODUCE* the concept of brainstorming, by summarizing the guidelines on the first page of the *Brainstorming* handout. Use the *Brainstorming* overhead to show that brainstorming is supposed to be fun.

2. *SAY:* I'm sure you've all been in brainstorming sessions in the past, but this will remind us of the guidelines that encourage a successful creative session.

   Brainstorming has been around since advertising executive Alex Osborne introduced it in the 1930s. This handout will serve as a resource to us now and in the future.

   Let's practice brainstorming. And since the topic for today is creativity, let's brainstorm a list of all the things we could each do to enhance our personal creative ability.

3. *ASK* for two volunteers, one to facilitate the brainstorming session and the second to hang the flipchart pages on the wall as you fill them.

   LIST the ideas on a flipchart page as fast as people say them. Allow 15–20 minutes for the idea generation. Ask for a volunteer to get them typed and distributed to the group.

Debrief

Brainstorming is a very useful tool for generating ideas. But do remember that a long list of ideas is useless unless something is done with it. Keep in mind the GOD principle: Generate, Organize and Decide. Generating is only one-third of your task. Next you must organize these ideas, and decide what you will do with them.

Options   You may substitute another brainstorming topic for the one above.

- Use some of the variation on the second page of the *Brainstorming* handout.

- Use this as a warm-up before an actual brainstorming session.

TRAINER'S NOTES

<u>TRAINER'S NOTES</u>   **Lighting Others' Creativity**

Objective   To help participants see that they can assist others to be creative.

Time   • 15–20 minutes.

Materials   • Handout *Lighting Others' Creativity* (pp. 174-175).

                       • Overhead *Candle With Quote* (p. 278).

Procedure   1. *PROVIDE* participants with the *Lighting Others' Creativity* handout. Have participants read the quotes and complete the questions.

   2. *ASK:*

                       • Who would like to share their thoughts about this handout?

                       • Who can you encourage to be more creative?

                       • Any ideas about how you might do that?

                       • Other thoughts?

Debrief   *SUMMARIZE* the activity using the overhead, *Candle With Quote* and *SAY:*

   You have the opportunity to light others' creativity. You are both the candle and the mirror, able to light the creativity of those you touch.

Notes   • _____

                       • _____

                       • _____

                       • _____

                       • _____

                       • _____

                       • _____

                       • _____

                       • _____

                       • _____

                       • _____

                       • _____

<u>**Trainer's Notes**</u>	**The Five R's of Creativity**
Objective	To introduce participants to a five-step process of creative development and to use the five-step process to address an actual problem.
Time	• 60 minutes.
Materials	• Handout *The Five R's of Creativity* (p. 187).
	• Handout *The Steps in the Creative Process* (pp. 188-189).
	• Overhead *The Five R's of Creativity* (pp. 282-283).
Pre-work	Participants should come prepared to discuss a project, idea or problem they would like to explore using the creative process.

Procedure

1. *OPEN* by saying that creativity, is a process that you can follow and use successfully, just like any process you use on the job.

    Add that creativity does not happen magically; it is the result of a process—a system of thinking. There are five steps in the creative process. Just as there are the three R's (reading, 'riting and 'rithmetic.) Each step in the process starts with the letter "R".

2. *HAVE* participants arrange themselves in trios.

3. *PROVIDE* participants with *The Five R's of Creativity* handout. Tell them to work together in trios to number in sequence the five R's of creativity. Then connect the numbers in sequence to uncover their pattern.

4. *OBSERVE* the groups' progress as you walk around the room. Help out when needed. Once the groups have completed the activity, let them know that each step will be explored in detail.

5. *USE The Five R's of Creativity* overheads to illustrate the pattern.

6. *ASK* if they believe that the shape is significant? (Some will arrive at the sequence creatively, by connecting the points first. Praise this as creativity—remember, there are no rules.)

7. *DISCUSS* the following quotation by Tris Speaker:

> *"Ruth made a big mistake when he gave up pitching."*
>
> —Tris Speaker
> (1921, American baseball player in the Hall of Fame.
> Batting average of .344.)

Steps in the Creative Process

1. *PROVIDE* the participants with the *The Steps in the Creative Process* handout (pp. 188-189) and tell them to begin to work through the five–step process using the situation that each was asked to bring to this workshop.

First "R"   **Realize the Need**

a. Look at the first step in the creative process and *ASK* what they think it means.

b. *SAY* that many creative ideas, projects and products were not "needed" until "discovered." For instance, some came about as mistakes (e.g., Post-it Notes). Others were found accidentally (e.g., penicillin). Some came at odd times (e.g., at breakfast a waffle became the model for the Nike shoe sole).

c. *ASK* if they know of any other accidental discovery stories?

d. *SAY:* Using the problem that you brought to the session, create a specific objective that summarizes what the result should be. Be prepared to share your objective with the larger group. Get feedback from the other two people in your trio.

e. *SAY:* You will have five minutes to write your objective statement. *ASK* them to share their objectives and close this activity by making these points about the objectives:

   - They must be stated clearly and specifically.

   - They must be measurable.

   - They must meet the need.

Second "R"   **Review the Data**

a. *SAY* that the second step in the creative process is to review all of the data available to you. Have them read the introductory remarks to step 2 and complete this activity individually.

SAY: We must continue to put information into our brain. We can organize it and arrange it later.

b. Give them time to complete this step and have several share their resources and sources. *CLOSE* by adding any unmentioned resources that you have noted for your company.

239

Third "R"   **Rest the Data**

a. *SAY*: once you have thoroughly reviewed the data, let it rest. The third step in the creative process is to rest the data.

b. *LEAD* a discussion around step 3 and add the following information on dreaming:

1. Keep pen and paper by your bed with light available.

2. Record your dreams, looking for patterns and re-occurrences.

3. Place a tape recorder by your bed.

4. Just before falling asleep, give yourself a mental suggestion that you will remember what you dream.

5. Before sleeping, think of a problem like a metaphor. The subconscious "likes" metaphors. Ask your subconscious for a solution.

6. If you talk in your sleep have someone awaken you.

c. *ASK* for a volunteer to share an instance where resting the data or dreaming on it paid off. Be prepared to offer your own example.

Fourth "R"   **Recognize the Spark**

a. *SAY:* if you have performed the first three steps, the fourth will come on its own. Be prepared to recognize and capture the spark or idea or inspiration, or whatever you call the creative moment, when it hits you.

b. *REVIEW* the introductory remarks with them and have them complete the activity in their trios.

c. *PROCESS* this activity. Use a round robin to share their methods for capturing ideas with the larger group. Be prepared to add onto their lists with these:

- Keep a running note pad.
- Take notes while reading.
- Ask a person to awaken you if you talk in your sleep.
- Repeat the information three times.
- Review the notes daily.
- Use association with objects or words.
- Tell another person.
- Methods unique to your organization, (e.g., dictation available 24 hours by phone, hand-held Dictaphone, personal computers at work and home).

Fifth "R"   **Refine**

    a. *SAY:* The last step in the creative process is to refine. If you do not perform this last step, your creative spark may die out from lack of polishing.

    b. *READ* the introductory remarks and review the JUDGE process by making these points:

Justify

Justify its existence (positives). List all of the good things about your idea. Why is it good? What good will it create?

Undermine

Undermine its development (negatives). Now, list all of the reasons why your idea will not work. Play your own devil's advocate.

Delay

Delay your personal biases and attitudes (be neutral). Keep yourself from judging the idea too quickly. Stop yourself from making a decision at this time. Do not be hasty.

Generate

Generate the decision (use a process). Use a decision-making tool that has worked for you in the past. (Be prepared to insert information on the specific kinds of decision-making tools and processes that are used at your company. You may discuss consensus, expert, authority rule with discussion, majority vote, minority control or any other decision-making methods that will be familiar to the participants. What about a coin toss?)

Execute

Execute your decision (action). Do it! Ideas are worthless on the drawing board. Plan for the budget, anticipate objections, draw up a schedule, prepare an action plan and determine a contingency plan.

    c. *HAVE* them work in their trios to JUDGE this idea: Winning is everything.

    d. When they have completed the activity, *ASK* for the results from each group.

Debrief *SUMMARIZE* the activity by saying that we've reached the end, and that you hope they have accomplished two things:

- Have some ideas in general about how to use the five–step creative process.

- Have an idea or two about their specific situations.

Notes

- _____

- _____

- _____

- _____

- _____

- _____

- _____

- _____

- _____

- _____

- _____

- _____

- _____

- _____

- _____

- _____

- _____

- _____

- _____

- _____

- _____

- _____

- _____

Optional Activities

Eyedeas Energizer

Objective

To provide an energizing break during a creativity (or any other) workshop, to introduce participants to the concept of seeing things from a different perspective and to get participants to practice with a right brain activity.

Time

- 10 minutes.

Materials

- Handout *Eyedeas* (p. 190).

Procedure

1. *REFER* to *Eyedeas* handout and *ASK* participants to work with a partner to think of as many things as possible that these eyedeas can be while you time them for three minutes. Tell them to question why they are doing this activity as they perform the task. What does this have to do with creativity?

2. When completed, *ASK* how many responses each group thought of.

3. *USE* a modified round robin to get some of the ideas out. Note that you will not have time to hear all the ideas from everyone.

Debrief

To debrief *ASK* what this activity has to do with creativity? Make these points in the discussion:

- It's making sense out of nonsense.

- It's seeing things from different perspectives.

- It demonstrates more than one right answer.

Notes

- _____

- _____

- _____

- _____

- _____

- _____

- _____

- _____

- _____

**TRAINER'S NOTES**   **Your Creative Style**

Objective

To assist participants to identify their creative style preferences and to address some advantages and potential problems each creative style preference presents.

Time

- 40–90 minutes (depends on the questionnaire used).

Materials

- Handout *Your Creative Style* (p. 191).

- Self-assessment questionnaire of your choice to identify creative style (see Appedix pp. 292-293).

Procedure

1. *DISTRIBUTE* a questionnaire to each participant. Explain the instructions and instruct them to complete and score it. Give them time to do so. This will probably take 10–20 minutes.

   Several self-assessment questionnaires are listed in the appendix. Choose the one that meets your needs. *Your Creative Style* handout asks participants to explore their attributes and the advantages and problems their style may present. Use the handout as long as it matches the instrument you have chosen.

2. When you see that everyone has completed scoring, have them break into groups based on how they scored—according to their description.

   Have them discuss in their groups and record:

   - Those attributes which describe them.

   - The advantages of these descriptors.

   - The possible problems of these descriptors.

3. *HAVE* the sub-groups report to the larger group.

4. *FACILITATE* the discussion based on the participant's questions and concerns. The goal of this discussion should be clearer understanding of each of the styles.

Debrief

SUMMARIZE by saying that no matter what your creative style happens to be, everyone can see that they are all necessary to generate the best ideas and to make the best decisions.

<u>**TRAINER'S NOTES**</u>	**Kid's Game Energizer**
Objective	To provide a quick energizer between activities of any kind, to introduce a very simple right-brain thinking activity, and to introduce the combine creativity technique.
Time	• 10–20 minutes.
Materials	• Handout *Kid's Game* (p. 192).
	• Flipchart and pen.

Procedure

1. ***TELL*** participants that you are going to introduce a creativity technique called combine.

2. To put them into small groups:

   • Have them list five favorite games as a large group. First five named are written on the flipchart.

   • Assign a game name to five different places in the room.

   • Have participants go to the spot of their favorite game.

3. ***TELL*** them that they are going to use another favorite game, Monopoly, to enhance their next staff meeting.

4. Each team is asked to list ways they could use the elements and rules of Monopoly to facilitate their next staff meeting.

5. Assign the amount of time based on your expectations of this activity.

6. ***CALL*** time.

Debrief   Use the ideas from the activity as a summary.

Notes

• _____

• _____

• _____

• _____

• _____

• _____

• _____

• _____

<u>**TRAINER'S NOTES**</u>   **Characteristics of Creative People**

Objective   To identify characteristics of creative people.

Time   • 20–30 minutes.

Materials   • None.

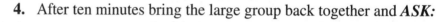

Procedure 1. *OPEN* the activity by stating that everyone has the potential to be creative. Yet wouldn't it be interesting to identify characteristics of those people that we judge to be at the most creative end of the creative spectrum?

   2. *HAVE* participants individually generate a list of characteristics of creative people they have known.

   3. *FORM* small groups of four to five people in each and have them compare lists.

   4. After ten minutes bring the large group back together and *ASK:*

   • What did you find? Similarities? Dissimilarities?

   • What does this tell you about creative people?

   Some of the characteristics that might be mentioned include:

   • Driven.

   • Different.

   • Fun-loving.

   • Don't follow rules.

   • Spontaneous.

   • Independent.

   • Enthusiastic.

   • Sensitive to their own senses
     (sight, smell, sound, touch, taste).

   • See things where others don't.

   • Take action.

   • Push beyond obstacles.

   • Not content with the obvious.

In addition, some of the words that they have listed may be exact opposites:

- Patient and impatient.

- Bold and timid.

- Funny and serious.

- Accurate and approximate.

- Punctual and late.

- Proper and informal.

- Detail-oriented and big picture-oriented.

This simply demonstrates that all of you—no matter what your personality—have the ability to be creative.

5. You may wish to provide the following information: studies of famous people (e.g., Edison, Einstein, Ford, Franklin), known for their creative abilities, do have some characteristics in common. Some of these might surprise you:

    - Many of them did not do well in the traditional educational structure. Many did not attend or complete college.

    - They are a social bunch who thrive on visiting and talking with other people.

    - They don't give up, and they are highly motivated.

    - They worked long and hard in their field before they created something for which they are renowned.

    - Their early experiences were varied and filled with the freedom to explore.

    - They have excellent senses of humor.

Debrief   Bring the activity to a close by *ASKING:* What does this tell you about your creativity?

Notes

- _____

- _____

- _____

- _____

- _____

- _____

<u>**Trainer's Notes**</u>	**Left-Brain/Right-Brain Shift**
Objective	To provide an opportunity for people to experience a shift from one brain style to the other.
Time	• 20–40 minutes.
Materials	• Paper.

Procedure

1. *SAY:* an easy way to experience a shift from one brain style to another is through drawing. When drawing an object you view right side up, you use the left side of your brain.

2. *ALLOW* participants to choose a line drawing that they would like to duplicate.

3. Wait until they have drawn the figure. Then *SAY:* now take another sheet of paper, turn the picture upside down and draw the same illustration.

4. Give them time to draw. When they have completed, *ASK*: how did these two drawings differ for you?

5. Make the following points during the discussion:

   a. Drawing the illustration right side up was a left-brained activity. It was probably drawn one piece at a time, naming them one by one. (e.g., right side, left side, outline head, eyebrows, eyes, nose, add flower.)

   b. Drawing the illustration upside down was a right-brained activity. It was probably drawn using spatial, relational and comparative cues.

   c. If a participant felt uncomfortable using the right-brained approach (the illustration was upside down) this could be explained by the fact that the participant was trying to use a left-brained approach to a right-brained problem.

   d. Usually, the second drawing (right-brained, viewed upside down) looks better than the left-brained, or first drawing.

   e. Creating the second drawing should have "felt" different. There is a cognitive shift from left-brained thinking to right-brained thinking—just as we shift in and out of daydreams.

Debrief

Summarize the differences by referring to words that describe the two thinking styles: right-brain thinking (intuitive, visual, timeless, subjective, spontaneous, emotional) and left-brain thinking (analytical, verbal, sequential, objective, cause and effect, logical).

Creative Reading Project

Objective

To introduce participants to topics related to creativity.

Time

- 10 minutes to select a book and 20 minutes to debrief. (This activity requires time between sessions to read or scan the chosen book.)

Materials

- A selection of books.

Procedure [?]

1. *ASK* participants to take the next ten minutes to select a book as a project before the next session. The only criterion is that they select a type of book that they have never read. Ask them to sign a sign-out sheet so you may keep track of the books. Let them know that (depending on the timing between sessions) they may skim, scan, browse through, or devour the book.

   Suggested topics to make available:

   - Mysticism.
   - Astral projection.
   - Philosophy.
   - ESP.
   - Inventions.
   - Mythology.
   - Poetry.
   - Psychology.
   - Biographies.
   - The brain.
   - Monsters.
   - Chaos theory.
   - Astrology/UFOs.
   - Science fiction.
   - Quantum physics.
   - Occult.
   - Motivational.
   - Positive thinking.
   - Light theory.
   - Color theory.
   - Art, drawing.
   - Brain teasers.
   - Story books (e.g., Arabian Nights).
   - Mind/Body connections.

[?]

2. Let participants know they will share their reading projects at their next session. At the next session, *ASK*:

   - Why did you make that selection?
   - What did you do with the book? (e.g., skimmed, read excerpts.)
   - Did you learn anything new? If so, what?
   - How did you feel about the experience?
   - Will you read more books like this one?

Debrief

CLOSE the discussion by saying:

Why did you do this? To expand your mind; to reach out to the unknown; to widen your spectrum. Reading new topics is only one way to keep a flow of new ideas coming. Be on the lookout for other ways to gather new information, to explore new worlds. Where do you get new ideas?

TRAINER'S NOTES   Signs of Creativity

Objective

To close a creativity session on an upbeat note and to "create" statements that summarize how to be more creative.

Time

- 15–20 minutes.

Materials

- Flipchart sheets for each small group.

- *Signs of Creativity* supplies for colorful signs:

    – Crayons.

    – Water colors.

    – Colored markers

- Prepared flipchart with "signs of creativity" quotes.

    The following sayings should be printed on flipchart pages and decorated with colorful borders, drawings or graphics.)

    – "All behavior consists of opposites. . . learn to see things backward, inside out and upside down." —Lao-tsu

    – "Think like nature. Ask: how would nature solve this problem?" —Jonas Salk

    – "Swipe from the best, then adapt." —Tom Peters

    – "Make friends with your shower. If inspired to sing, maybe the song has an idea in it for you." —Albert Einstein

Procedure

1. *SAY* that to close we'd like to create some reminders of how to be creative.

2. *DISPLAY* the "signs of creativity."

3. *SAY* that after working with creativity, participants will be able to create more colorful, more meaningful signs of creativity.

4. *HAVE* them form small groups to develop their own signs of creativity.

    Allow 10–12 minutes.

5. *HAVE* each group present their signs with much fanfare and applause.

Debrief

SEND the participants off with reminders to keep creativity in front of them. Creativity is a sign of progress, excitement and renewal.

Chapter Eight:

Measuring Creativity

It may seem strange to "measure creativity." Creativity is so, well, immeasurable! So right-brained! Yet most people love to measure things, to know how we stack up with others, with other companies.

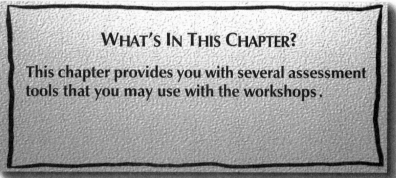

WHAT'S IN THIS CHAPTER?

This chapter provides you with several assessment tools that you may use with the workshops.

The Instruments Included

Needs Assessment

The first instrument in this chapter is a *Creativity Needs Assessment* (pp. 254-256). It can be used in a couple of ways.

1. You, as the facilitator, can use it as a workshop needs assessment. Send it out to future workshop participants. Use the results to:

    •   Tailor the workshop for your participants.

    •   Present the data as part of your workshop information.

    •   Present portions of the data during specific activities and create new activities around the data.

        For example, if a large number of participants believed that "management gets in the way of creativity. " You could have them brainstorm how to prevent it, or identify how resources, time or ideas are being lost.

Observe trends in the data as you facilitate more and more of the creativity workshops and present them to management.

2. Your organization may also wish to do a corporate-wide needs assessment that helps to pinpoint what the company should do to nurture the creative environment.

Creativity Climate Survey

The *Creativity Climate Survey* (pp. 257-261) is used in the one-day workshop as a discussion starter. However, it too, could be adapted for use with the entire organization. It provides results in six categories: how open-minded, perceptive, equal, nurturing, encouraging and descriptive the climate is. These six categories provide the basis for what is needed to foster a creative climate.

The *Creativity Climate Survey* provides a dual scoring system that measures the climate from the positive as well as the negative. The positive score is represented as an "open climate" score. The negative score is represented as a "closed climate" score.

In addition, the survey is accompanied by 29 ideas to encourage an open climate. These ideas are also used in the one-day session to help participants develop specific ways in which their organization (department or company as a whole) can open its climate to creativity.

Other Instruments You May Use

There are many other instruments that you may wish to use. Listed here are a few that we have used with success. Those from the *University Associates Annuals* (Pfeiffer and Company) are copyright-free if used within your organization for educational purposes. Others are inexpensive to purchase.

C&RT

The C&RT, which stands for creativity and risk taking, is designed to help members of a team explore characteristics that affect the way they contribute to the team's success. By plotting creativity against risk taking on a grid, the instrument places you in one of eight categories that describes your "creativity type." It provides a list of contributions and hindrances that each type displays. Good discussion starter for group work. The author is Richard E. Byrd. It can be purchased from Pfeiffer and Company, 619/578-2042.

Left-Brain/Right-Brain Self Assessments

We've used two in this category.

- *Orientations: Left-Brain/Right-Brain Problem Solving* by Daniel J. Nacht, Kurt Kraiger and Ruth Mandrell. It provides a way to measure an individual's dominance and describes how the different orientations affect the completion of a task. It also develops an understanding of the benefits and drawbacks of the different orientations. It can be found in the *1988 University Associates Annual* and can be copied and used internally. The annual is available from Pfeiffer and Company, 619/578-2042.

- *Self-Assessment of Brain Dominance and Energy* by Dr. Ann McGee-Cooper. This self-assessment identifies which activities energize you and which don't. From that you can identify your brain's dominance. This assessment has the potential to "revolutionize your ability to take full advantage of your brain's innate powers." The instrument can be found in *You Don't Have to Go Home from Work Exhausted!* by the same author. A quick and easy tool, creates good discussion, not validated. Published by Bowen and Rogers, this book is available by calling 800/477-8550.

**Inventory of Barriers
to Creative Thought and Innovative Action**

This thirty-six question assessment results in a list of scores in six barrier categories including self-confidence and risk taking, need to conform, use of the abstract, use of systematic analysis, task achievement and physical environment. It has a retest reliability of 89% and demonstrates construct and content validity. The author, Lorna P. Martin, also provides discussion starters for when the instrument is used in a group. It can be copied for use in your organization out of the *1990 University Associates Annual* available from Pfeiffer and Company, 619/578-2042.

Creativity Needs Assessment

Today's world of information explosions, quantum technological leaps, intense competition, higher quality expectations, shorter product life cycles demands new survival skills for American business. Innovation and creativity have been proclaimed as the basic skills required to be successful in a constantly changing world. Organizations that have supported creativity have been touted as models of success to improve performance and remain competitive.

Most recent literature supports the concept that innovation and creativity are important elements of a successful corporation: not just buzzwords, but basic survival skills. Innovation and creativity can take us down the road to competitive ability and future success.

How This Affects You

Corporate growth and a renewed emphasis on productivity will present new challenges and opportunities for (our company). Creativity training provides tools to help you meet these challenges, take advantage of the opportunities and adapt to the changes. In support of your creative work, you will be participating in a creativity workshop.

What to Do

Please take the time to complete the following two-page needs assessment. It could take you as little as ten minutes or as much as twenty-five minutes to finish it. Naturally, the more complete your responses, the more individualized the program will be to meet specific needs as perceived by you and your colleagues.

Please return this needs assessment to me within one week.

Creativity Needs Assessment

Your organizational level or title:

_____

How many years have you been with the company? _____

Directions   Measure the creativity climate in our company. Explore the four
               areas (Creativity; Creativity and Our Company; Risk Taking and
               Our Company; Creativity and You.) The statements in each area
               describe attitudes toward creativity. Read each statement and deter-
               mine to what degree it represents creativity attitudes to you.
               Respond using the following scale.

Answer key   1 = Strongly Disagree, 2 = Disagree, 3 = Somewhat Agree,
               4 = Agree, 5 = Strongly Agree

	Disagree				Agree

Creativity

1. Creativity is an inborn talent.	1	2	3	4	5
2. Creativity can be taught.	1	2	3	4	5
3. An individual's creativity can be improved.	1	2	3	4	5
4. Creativity is necessary in the workplace.	1	2	3	4	5
5. Creativity is linked to productivity.	1	2	3	4	5
6. Creativity is a waste of time.	1	2	3	4	5

What do you want to know about creativity?

Creativity and Our Company

1. Creativity is encouraged here.	1	2	3	4	5
2. Innovation is rewarded here.	1	2	3	4	5
3. Management gets in the way of creativity.	1	2	3	4	5
4. Employees are free to develop new ideas.	1	2	3	4	5
5. Our competition has more innovative ideas.	1	2	3	4	5
6. Our company is a creative organization.	1	2	3	4	5

How does our company encourage or stifle creativity?

Creativity Needs Assessment (cont.)

	Disagree			Agree	

Risk Taking and Our Company

1. Risk taking is encouraged here.	1	2	3	4	5
2. People are permitted to use their judgment.	1	2	3	4	5
3. Established practices can be challenged.	1	2	3	4	5
4. Failure and mistakes are acceptable.	1	2	3	4	5
5. Unconventional ideas get a fair hearing.	1	2	3	4	5

What must be changed here to increase risk taking?

Creativity and You

1. I enjoy looking for new ways to do things.	1	2	3	4	5
2. I wish I had more time to be creative.	1	2	3	4	5
3. I would like to increase my creative abilities.	1	2	3	4	5
4. I am willing to take a risk for a good idea.	1	2	3	4	5
5. I am creative.	1	2	3	4	5
6. Believing I am creative will make me more creative.	1	2	3	4	5

Your thoughts, ideas, or questions:

Creativity Climate Survey

Directions   Measure the creativity climate that you are working in today. Respond using the following scale.

Answer key   1 = Strongly Agree, 2 = Agree, 3 = Uncertain, 4 = Disagree, 5 = Strongly Disagree

		Agree				Disagree
1.	My work is criticized without letting me explain.	1	2	3	4	5
2.	I am encouraged to be as creative as possible.	1	2	3	4	5
3.	Management judges employees' actions.	1	2	3	4	5
4.	Management allows flexibility on the job.	1	2	3	4	5
5.	New ideas are not valued in this job.	1	2	3	4	5
6.	Management is open to new ideas and change.	1	2	3	4	5
7.	My manager controls how or when I do my work.	1	2	3	4	5
8.	My manager understands the problems that I handle in my job.	1	2	3	4	5
9.	Management shows little respect or interest in new ideas.	1	2	3	4	5
10.	My manager respects my feelings, values and ideas.	1	2	3	4	5
11.	Little flexibility exists in the work environment.	1	2	3	4	5
12.	My manager protects my creative ideas.	1	2	3	4	5
13.	My ideas have been presented as someone else's ideas.	1	2	3	4	5
14.	I am respected for the diversity I bring.	1	2	3	4	5
15.	I have to be careful in talking with management so I will be understood.	1	2	3	4	5
16.	Management interacts with employees without projecting higher status or power.	1	2	3	4	5
17.	Management takes credit for employees' ideas.	1	2	3	4	5
18.	My manager respects and trusts me.	1	2	3	4	5
19.	Management is not open with information.	1	2	3	4	5
20.	I am provided opportunities to learn and experience new things.	1	2	3	4	5
21.	Management treats everyone the same.	1	2	3	4	5

22.	The organization's climate stimulates creativity.	1	2	3	4	5
23.	My manager rarely gives moral support to employees.	1	2	3	4	5
24.	I can express my ideas openly and honestly to my manager.	1	2	3	4	5
25.	Sometimes I feel powerless and inadequate.	1	2	3	4	5
26.	My manager communicates ideas so that they can be understood but does not insist that I agree.	1	2	3	4	5
27.	My manager makes it clear who is the boss.	1	2	3	4	5
28.	I have time and resources to be creative.	1	2	3	4	5
29.	Management checks everything to ensure that work is done right.	1	2	3	4	5
30.	I am rewarded for taking appropriate risks.	1	2	3	4	5
31.	Management cannot admit to mistakes.	1	2	3	4	5
32.	Management describes situations clearly and objectively.	1	2	3	4	5
33.	My manager is dogmatic; I can't change my manager's mind.	1	2	3	4	5
34.	My manager provides appropriate direction and feedback.	1	2	3	4	5
35.	Management thinks that their ideas are always correct.	1	2	3	4	5
36.	I am encouraged to have direct customer contact.	1	2	3	4	5

> "The future belongs to those societies that. . .enable the characteristically human elements of our nature to flourish, to those societies that encourage diversity rather than conformity."
>
> —Carl Sagan

Creativity Climate Survey Scoring

Put the numbers you assigned to each statement in the appropriate blanks. Add them to subtotal each climate descriptor. Add together the subtotals in each column to obtain the final scores.

1. _____ **C**ritical

3. _____

5. _____

Subtotal _____

7. _____ **L**ashing

9. _____

11. _____

Subtotal _____

13. _____ **O**pportunistic

15. _____

17. _____

Subtotal _____

19. _____ **S**olo

21. _____

23. _____

Subtotal _____

25. _____ **E**gotistical

27. _____

29. _____

Subtotal _____

31. _____ **D**ogmatic

33. _____

35. _____

Subtotal _____

Closed Score _____

2. _____ **O**pen-minded

4. _____

6. _____

Subtotal _____

8. _____ **P**erceptive

10. _____

12. _____

Subtotal _____

14. _____ **E**qual

16.

18. _____

Subtotal _____

20. _____ **N**urturing

22. _____

24. _____

Subtotal _____

26. _____ **E**ncouraging

28. _____

30. _____

Subtotal _____

32. _____ **D**escriptive

34. _____

36. _____

Subtotal _____

Opened Score _____

Total Score Guide

No matter what your climate score or label is, you are now aware of your climate's tone. This can provide the information and foundation to foster improving your creativity climate.

Closed		**Opened**	
18 – 41	Closed	18 – 41	Opened
42 – 65	Neutral	42 – 65	Neutral
66 – 90	Opened	66 – 90	Closed

Opened Climates

Open-minded

Encourage flexibility and creativity.

1. Allow employees to schedule their own work and deadlines as much as possible.

2. Allow employees to experiment with using creative approaches and techniques.

3. See employees as creative people by recognizing creative efforts.

4. Encourage total group involvement in creative efforts by establishing work teams.

5. Budget for creative efforts.

Perceptive

See things from your employees' viewpoint.

1. Ensure that the work is rewarding both in a professional and personal way (e.g., interesting and significant).

2. Encourage a participative atmosphere by asking for and acting upon employees' input.

3. Protect creative employees' from dullards who don't understand what makes them tick.

4. Be a role model who is creative.

5. Minimize the risk factors and share the responsibility (e.g., giving research time).

Equal

Respect everyone for the diversity each brings.

1. Give employees credit by implementing ideas without editing or changing them.

2. Enter employees' work in competition.

3. Ensure that ideas are implemented well.

4. Individualize leadership techniques and styles that fit the needs of each employee.

Nurturing

Stimulate free expression of ideas.

1. Listen to creative ideas with interest.

2. Provide creative pollen through speakers and other learning opportunities.

3. Foster creativity in group work as well as in individual projects.

4. Provide the necessary climate stimulus (e.g., a creative room, purple office, quiet space or whatever it takes).

5. Accommodate regeneration needs through paid time off, sabbaticals, etc.

Encouraging

Encourage employees to find answers creatively.

1. Provide the time needed to do so by delaying other work or delegating to another person.

2. Open up resources and avenues for exploration.

3. Serve as a catalyst with actions (not just words) to employees' creative endeavors (e.g., get them what they need).

4. Positively reinforce and reward risks.

5. Allow freedom and opportunity for self-expression.

6. Identify those who exhibit creativity and select them as mentors.

D

Descriptive

Give clear objectives and specific feedback.

1. State the purpose of the task in specific—not vague—terms.

2. Balance structure with opportunity for creative expression.

3. Provide input through direct customer contact.

4. Give explicit, as well as supporting, feedback.

Chapter Nine:

Overhead Transparencies

Preparing overhead transparencies, flipcharts, and other visual aids is a time consuming but rewarding part of your work as a creativity training professional. This chapter contains the masters which will make your job a breeze.

WHAT'S IN THIS CHAPTER?

This chapter contains the masters for the following visual aids, to give your training session a professional appearance:

- Overhead transparencies.

- Group table tents.

- Turtle award.

Presentation Tips

Overhead transparencies

There are a total of 19 overhead transparency masters, 17 of which are used in the one-day workshop. Make one of each. They are ready for immediate photocopying onto acetates. We recommend that you "make them colorful" by coloring them with a permanent marker or adding self-adhering colored film. They could also be scanned into your computer, colored, and printed on a color printer or sent to a desktop publishing service bureau. *Creativity Techniques*, the light bulb graphic, can be enhanced very easily by just copying it directly onto a yellow acetate.

If you wish, professionally colored transparencies are available. Information can be found in the appendix section.

For a professional appearance, be sure to put them into transparency frames before you use them. Large cardboard frames work well for adding your own training notes. Most recently, many facilitators use the 3M flip frames. They clean up the edges nicely, yet can be stored in a three-ring binder with your training materials. (These differ from page protectors, which do not enhance overhead transparency appearance.)

To ensure that your participants get the most from the transparencies:

- Wash the overhead projector glass.

- Use a pointer on the projector (e.g., translucent colored stir stick, appetizer pick or a pencil) to focus participants' attention.

- Use a heavy piece of light colored paper for the revealing technique. Place the paper under the transparency so that it won't fall off the projector as you move it down, and so you will be able to see what is coming next before the participants.

If an overhead projector is not available (perhaps your bulb burns out and you don't have a spare, or perhaps you are conducting the session on the beach) you may transcribe the information onto flip charts. You will still have the visuals in front of the group.

These overhead transparencies have been designed as transparencies, not handouts. And as any good trainer knows, they are different. Therefore, we do not recommend that you photocopy them on paper as handouts.

Group table tents (pp. 284-288)

These are used to divide the participants into small groups. In both the one-day and the half-day workshop it is suggested to use all five. Of course, you may choose to use fewer.

We suggest that you copy them onto card stock and then color them with markers. You may wish to laminate them for protection. They are a small way that you display your professionalism and that you model the creativity techniques you are teaching others.

Turtle award

You will use these as awards for participants who "took a risk to lunch." Be generous with them.

We suggest that you run them on high quality parchment. The thought of a Turtle Award on parchment is so incongruous that it twists people's minds, which is exactly what you are trying to do in the creativity workshops—get them to think differently.

To make it official, the awards should be signed and dated by the facilitator(s).

Be creative!

DEFINE CREATIVITY

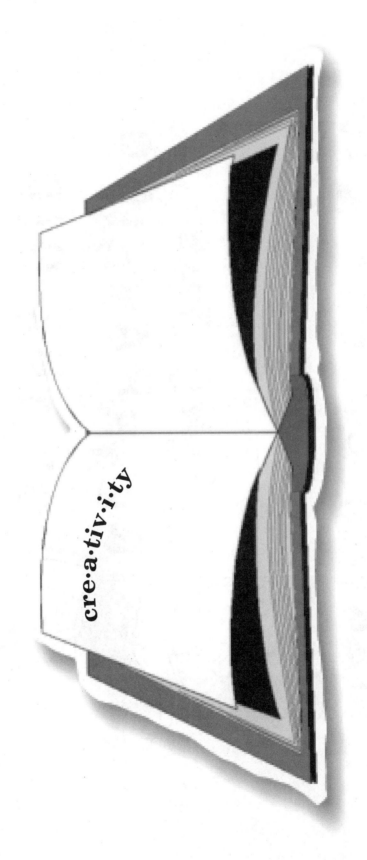

cre·a·tiv·i·ty

MAKING OF THE NEW

AND THE REARRANGING OF THE OLD

RIGHT-BRAIN/LEFT-BRAIN?

ANALYTICAL

VERBAL

SEQUENTIAL

OBJECTIVE

CAUSE & EFFECT

SCIENCE & MATH

LOGICAL

$E = mc^2$

$2y + 3x = 4z$

INTUITIVE

TIMELESS

VISUAL

SUBJECTIVE

SPONTANEOUS

ARTS & MUSIC

EMOTIONAL

WHOLE-BRAIN THINKING

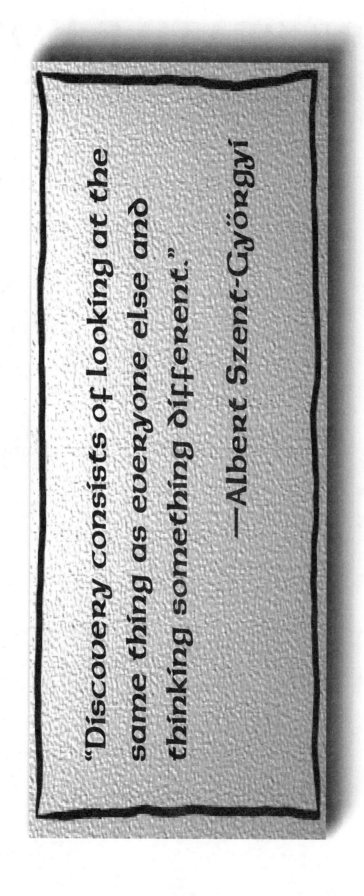

"Discovery consists of looking at the same thing as everyone else and thinking something different."

—Albert Szent-Györgyi

NINE UNCREATIVE BOXES

Time Trapped

Environmental Pollution

Risky Business Zone

Perfectionist Problem

Calm Waters

Wright or Wrong Thinking

Self-Fulfilling Prophecy

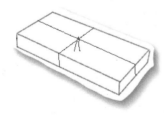

Only One Right Answer

Bottom-Line Thinking

UNBOX YOUR CREATIVITY

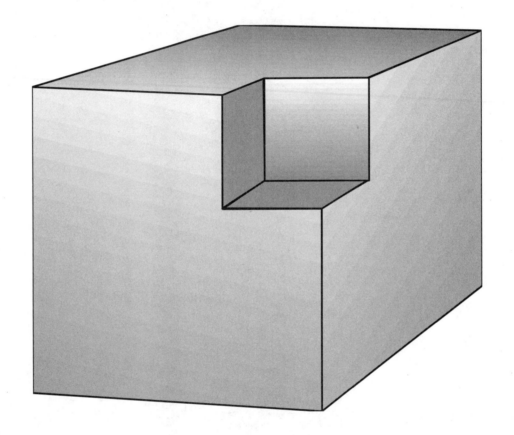

A SPECTRUM OF CREATIVITY TECHNIQUES

C ompare and combine

R isk taking

E xpand and shrink

A sk "What's good?" and "What if?"

T ransform your viewpoint

I n another sequence

V isit other places

I ncubate

T rigger concepts

Y outh's advantage

TURTLE RACE

"Behold the turtle.
He makes progress only when he
sticks his neck out."

—James Conan Bryant

THE COMPANY'S CREATIVE PAST

WHERE CAN CREATIVITY FLOURISH?

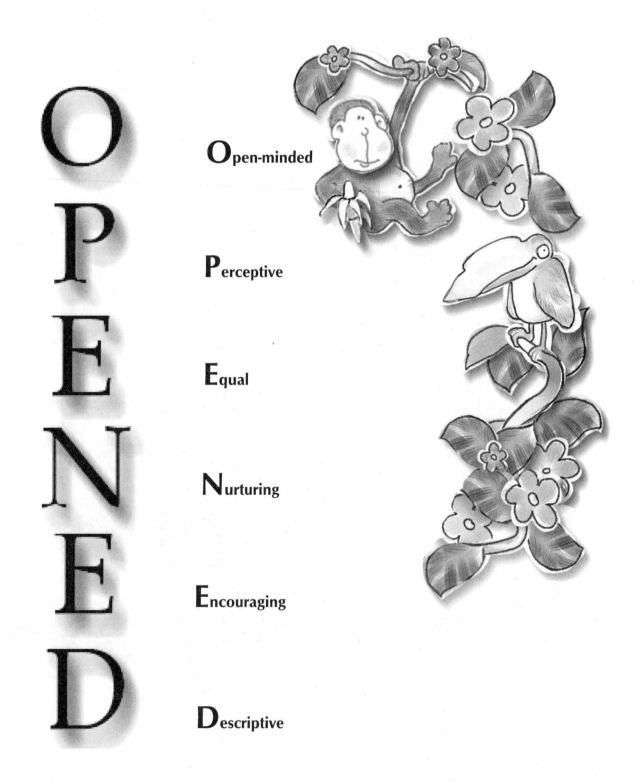

O

P

E

N

E

D

Open-minded

Perceptive

Equal

Nurturing

Encouraging

Descriptive

BRAINSTORMING

Better to light one candle than to curse the darkness.

CREATIVE FLASHES

COME OUT OF YOUR
SHELL

FLOWER

THE FIVE R'S OF CREATIVITY

___ Review the data

___ Refine
(connect to #1)

Recognize the spark ___

___ Rest the data

___ Realize the need

THE FIVE R'S OF CREATIVITY

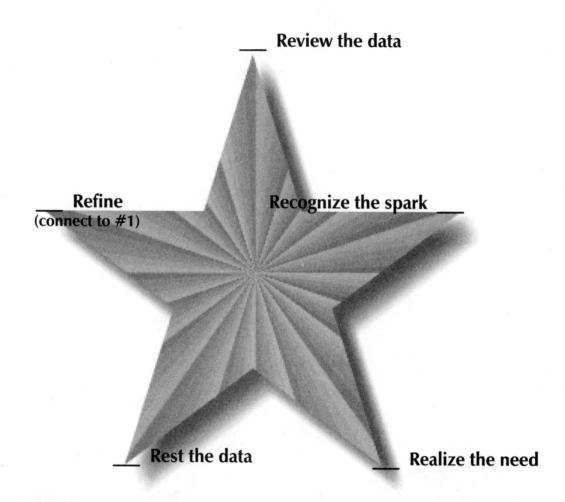

___ Review the data

___ Refine
(connect to #1)

Recognize the spark ___

___ Rest the data

___ Realize the need

Likes to play with clay

Would like to write a book

Has painted
a picture

Enjoys daydreaming

Is a
"closet poet"

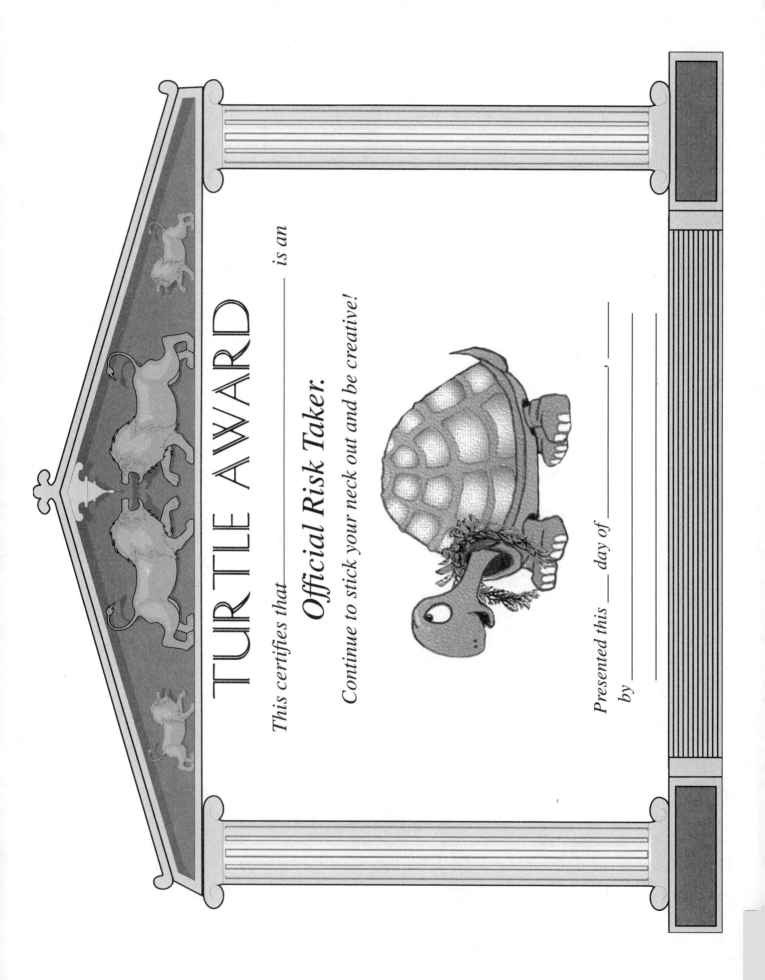

TURTLE AWARD

This certifies that _____ is an

Official Risk Taker.

Continue to stick your neck out and be creative!

Presented this _____ day of _____, _____

by _____

Recommended Resources

Creativity Tools

Idea Sparker Cards

Can be given to participants at the beginning of the workshop and used throughout or can be given at the end as a reminder of the experience. Following the session, they will have creativity sparker activities to use at their desks. The 56 business card-size activities come in a desk-top holder and provide ten minute exercises to be used daily to stimulate right-brain thinking. Available from ebb associates, Box 657, Portage, WI 53901, 800/ebb-9-ebb.

Pocket Innovator

A hand-held creativity tool, similar to colored paint chips, combining hundreds of key words with a seven-stage Creative Development Process and Mini-Ideas Library. It will help you brainstorm a high volume and wide variety of quality ideas, solve problems, and improve your creative thinking skills. Designed by Karen Koberg and Gerald Haman, and available from Creative Learning International, Box 13601, Minneapolis, MN 55414, 612/379-4427.

Creative Whack Pack

This is a creativity tool that will "whack" you out of habitual thought patterns and allow you to look at what you're doing in a fresh way. It consists of 64 cards each bearing a different creativity principle. Can be used alone or with others as a mental stimulant, a creativity workshop, a guide to the creativity process and as an oracle. Designed by Roger von Oech, author of *A Whack on the Side of the Head*, the card deck is available from Creative Think, Box 7354, Menlo Park, CA 94026, 415/321-6775.

Thinkpak

56 idea-stimulating cards to get you started right away generating dozens and dozens of creative new ideas. An excellent brainstorming tool designed to change the way you think and produce a wide variety of fresh thoughts that will lead to new insights, original ideas and creative solutions to problems. Designed by Michael Michalko, author of *Thinkertoys*, the card deck is available from Ten Speed Press, Box 7123, Berkeley, CA 94707, 800/841-BOOK.

Session Enhancements

Music

Music is protected by copyright. You may obtain copyright-free music from Bob Pike, Resources for Organization, 7620 West 78th Street, Bloomington, MN 55439, 800/383-9210.

"Road to Success" Slides

Will enhance the script in module three of the one-day workshop. The set of 39 slides begins bright and colorful, then subtly becomes darker and grayer as the script moves along. Tap into participants' visual learning mode. For information about slides available from ebb associates, call 800/ebb-9-ebb.

Overhead Transparencies

Set of 19 computer colored overhead transparencies, framed and ready-to-go. For information about slides available from ebb associates, call 800/ebb-9-ebb.

Instruments and Assessments

Listed below are a few instruments we have used with success. Those from the *University Associates Annuals* are copyright-free if used within your organization for educational purposes. Others are inexpensive to purchase.

C&RT
by Richard E. Byrd

The *C&RT*, which stands for creativity and risk taking, helps members of a team explore characteristics that affect the way they contribute to the team's success. By plotting creativity against risk taking on a grid, the instrument places you in one of eight categories that describe your "creativity type." It provides a list of contributions and hindrances that each type displays. Good discussion starter for group work. It can be purchased from Pfeiffer and Company, 619/578-2042.

Left/right brain self assessments

Orientations: Left-Brain/Right-Brain Problem Solving
by Daniel J. Nacht, Kurt Kraiger and Ruth Mandrell

Provides a way to measure individuals dominance and describes how the different orientations affect the completion of a task. It also develops an understanding of the benefits and drawbacks of the different orientations. It can be found in the *1988 University Associates Annual* and can be copied and used internally. The annual is available from Pfeiffer and Company, 619/578-2042.

Self-Assessment of Brain Dominance and Energy
by Dr. Ann McGee-Cooper

This self-assessment identifies which activities energize you and which don't. From this instrument you can identify your brain's dominance and the potential to "revolutionize your ability to take full advantage of your brain's innate powers". The instrument can be found in *You Don't Have to Go Home from Work Exhausted!* by the same author. A quick and easy tool, creates good discussion, but is not validated. Published by Bowen and Rogers, this book is available by calling 800/477-8550.

Inventory of Barriers to Creative Thought and Innovative Action
by Lorna P. Martin

This 36 question assessment results in a list of scores in six barrier categories including self-confidence and risk taking, need to conform, use of the abstract, use of systematic analysis, task achievement and physical environment. It has a retest reliability of .89 and demonstrates construct and content validity. The author provides discussion starters when the instrument is used in a group. It can be copied for use in your organization out of the *1990 University Associates Annual*, available from Pfeiffer and Company. Call 619/578-2042.

Reading and Resource List

All of the following books are readily available from your library or bookstore. Some are new, others are classics. The various books provide techniques as well as theory and examples. All are fun to read. The three categories include creativity techniques, positive thinking and the brain.

Creativity techniques

Six Thinking Hats
by Edward de Bono

Shows how to break down our thinking process in more defined terms; allowing us to redirect our thinking as it pertains to different situations.

Thinkertoys
by Michael Michalko

A book designed to change the way you think. This fun-to-read book helps you use a variety of techniques to create and act on ideas.

301 Great Management Ideas from

America's Most Innovative Small Companies
by Sara Noble

The author has gathered ideas from several small companies and compiled them in an easy to read book. Many ideas can easily be implemented in your organization to benefit your company.

A Kick in the Seat of the Pants
by Roger von Oech

Defines four roles of the creative process. Practical approaches to becoming more innovative by using your explorer, artist, judge and warrior.

A Whack on the Side of the Head
by Roger von Oech

This well known classic breaks through old thinking patterns with tips, techniques and case histories to get ideas through play. Will unlock your mind for innovation.

Wake Up Your Creative Genius
by Kurt Hanks and Jay Parry

Use this as a source book for ideas, techniques and examples to get your creative juices flowing; it's entertaining and stimulating. Excellent resource for the trainer who wants additional ideas to design creativity training modules.

Why Didn't I Think of That?
by Roger L. Firestien

This fable provides ten points to make your imagination work for you. Helps you create better ideas and make better decisions in your personal and professional life.

Thunderbolt Thinking
by Grace McGartland

Shows you how to transform your insights and options into powerful business results. The book is filled with examples from other companies and features T•N•Ts (tips and techniques), to "craft breakthrough solutions" for your toughest problems.

So You've Got a Great Idea
by Steve Fiffer

Shows you how to develop, sell, market, or just cash in on those "great ideas."

99% Inspiration
by Bryan W. Mattimore

Will help you tap hidden creative strengths and shed new light on a wide range of issues affecting today's workforce. Many tips, tricks and techniques make this a good resource.

101 Creative Problem Solving Techniques
by James M. Higgins

A practical guide for putting creativity into your problem solving process. It's fun and entertaining with lots of practical applications for today's diverse work environment.

C And The Box
by Frank A. Prince

A ten-minute read that sends a powerful message with a delightful fantasy and an important reminder about the importance of thinking outside the box. Provide this to participants before your training to pique their interest.

Positive thinking

Ageless Body Timeless Mind
by Deepak Chopra

An inspiring book which looks at the body-mind connection. Redefines assumptions about aging and health with new unconventional thinking.

Feel the Fear and Do It Anyway
by Susan Jeffers, Ph.D.

Practical guidance to acknowledge your fears and turn them into positive action. Will help you make better decisions in all aspects of your life.

The Magic of Believing
by Claude M. Bristol

This classic tells you how to harness the unlimited energies of your subconscious mind. Make yourself more competent in your affairs, more influential in your dealings with others—in short, more successful in life.

Positive Imaging
by Norman Vincent Peale

Defines imaging and how to use it.   Gives you options to change and improve your life.

Rhinoceros Success
by Scott Alexander

A very unique look at charging up your inner strengths that will enable you to forge ahead in your life; not letting anything get in the way of your goals. A great motivator!

The brain

The Creative Brain
by Ned Herrmann

Revealing insight of overcoming traditional thinking with whole-brain concepts. It is user friendly with many insights and a multitude of applications.

Care and Feeding of the Brain
by Jack Maguire

Dubbed "a guide to your gray matter," this book tells you just about everything you'd want to know about the hows and whys of the human mind. It's provocative and enlightening.

ASTD Info–Lines

"Discovering and Developing Creativity"
by Stanley S. Gryskiewicz and Robert C. Preziosi, January 1989.

"Fifteen Activities to Discover and Develop Creativity"
by Stanley S. Gryskiewicz, Robert C. Preziosi and
Eugene Raudsepp, February 1989.

Brainstorming Software

Numerous software programs can be used to unleash creativity. The following sample programs are geared toward anyone whose work includes conceptualizing new ideas.

Idea Fisher

Contains a database of 65,000 words, which it links in 7,000,000 ways. Type the word "walk" and scores of vaguely related words and phrases appear: walk like an Egyptian; take the money and run. Available from Idea Fisher Systems, 800/289-4332.

Synchronicity

This system of applied wisdom will help you achieve clarity in understanding the reasons for your decisions. It will make decisions that logic alone can't handle, reduce stress, manage sensitive relationships and office politics, develop superior timing and access creative insight and intuitive power. Available from Visionary Software, Inc., 800/877-1832.

Inspiration

The program organizes chaotic user input into organized outline form. Available from Inspiration Software, 800/441-7234.

Idegen

Helps organize ideas, but sporadically throws out unrelated concepts to spur free-association. The user may be plotting a company strategy when a phrase such as "squirrel eating pine cones" appears. Available from Programmers Paradise, 800/445-7899.

Mindlink

Takes users on imaginary excursions. It asks you to imagine yourself in the jungle, or in a tree house, faced with the present situation. The theory, in its simplest terms, is that if you can be encouraged to think about a problem from a novel perspective, you may generate novel solutions. Available from Mindlink Software, 800/253-1844.

Video

Uncover Your Creativity

Zea, A Study in Perception

Creativity: The Only Way to Fly

These three videos are good session starters, team builders, energizers or could be used to give people a taste of creativity. Each is 5–8 minutes long and available for rent or purchase from Salinger Videos, 1635 12th Street, Santa Monica, CA 90404, 800/775-5025.

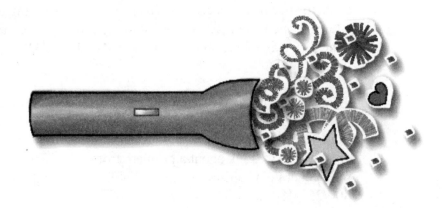

Free!

Set of Idea Sparkers

To order your free set of Idea Sparkers,
complete the information below and mail to:

ebb associates
Box 657
Portage, WI 53901

or fax to (608) 742-8657

Name _____

Title: _____

Organization: _____

Address: _____

City: _____ State: _____ Zip: _____

Telephone: _____ Fax: _____

ebb associates • box 657 • portage • wi • 53901
800/ebb-9-ebb or 800/322-9322

Index

About the Author

Elaine Biech is a founding partner of ebb associates inc, located in Portage, Wisconsin and Norfolk, Virginia. She has been in the training and consulting field for seventeen years. Known as the "trainer's trainer," she custom designs efforts that help people work together in teams to maximize their effectiveness. The author of numerous books and articles, Elaine holds a master's degree in Human Resource Development and has served as a member of the National Board of Directors for the American Society for Training and Development. In 1992, Elaine was awarded the ASTD Torch Award for excellence in her field.